# Father Knows Best

T0307882

## TV Milestones

*Series Editors*
Barry Keith Grant
Brock University

Jeannette Sloniowski
Brock University

*TV Milestones* is part of the Contemporary Approaches to Film and Media Series.

*A complete listing of the books in this series can be found online at wsupress.wayne.edu*

*General Editor*
Barry Keith Grant
Brock University

*Advisory Editors*
Robert J. Burgoyne
University of St. Andrews

Frances Gateward
California State University, Northridge

Caren J. Deming
University of Arizona

Tom Gunning
University of Chicago

Patricia B. Erens
School of the Art Institute of Chicago

Thomas Leitch
University of Delaware

Peter X. Feng
University of Delaware

Walter Metz
Southern Illinois University

Lucy Fischer
University of Pittsburgh

# FATHER KNOWS BEST

## Mary Desjardins

## TV MILESTONES SERIES

Wayne State University Press   Detroit

19 18 17 16 15          5 4 3 2 1

ISBN 978-0-8143-3947-3 (paperback) | ISBN 978-0-8143-3948-0 (ebook)

Library of Congress Control Number: 2015938131

To my brother Vincent, in memory of watching
TV reruns after school

# CONTENTS

vii

I have a very vague memory of watching *Father Knows Best* in one of its network prime-time broadcasts in the early 1960s. I would have been very young and watching with my family. I have much clearer memories a few years later of watching re-runs of *Father Knows Best* after school or during mornings when I stayed home sick. By the 1990s, I found the show a guilty pleasure when I tuned in to The Family Channel (a channel I would not ordinarily watch) at lunchtime while in my very first tenure-track teaching job in a city in which I didn't have many friends. And some years after that, *Father Knows Best* was a familiar comfort when I visited my mother and watched it in the assisted-living apartment that she lived in during the last few years of her life.

While it seemed inevitable that I would write about the series one day, I didn't anticipate other people's interest in and support of my project. Thanks to Wayne State University Press editors Kristina Stonehill and Annie Martin, who saw the book from proposal to final product. Kristina took me through the first part of the process while Annie was there at the end. I am particularly grateful for their patience with my delay in writing the first draft. Carrie Downes Teefey, assistant editorial manager at WSUP, has been a pleasure to work with as the manuscript made its way through production. I would also like to thank the two anonymous readers and TV Milestones series editors Barry Keith Grant and Jeannette Sloniowski for their helpful comments on the manuscript. I am grateful to Julie Graham, Accessioning Archivist, for her prompt and professional aid with the Eugene Rodney Collection at UCLA Library Special Collections. Peter Ciardelli, from my home Film and Media Studies Department at Dartmouth College, was an invaluable help with images, and his support always came with a smile. Thank you, Peter. Thanks to Jeremy Butler for making television style a scholarly priority in our field. Thanks also to Thomas Doherty for talking to me about the program when he visited Dartmouth and then following through later with some key information about Robert Young's political engagement.

A big thank-you goes to Barbara Hall for her friendship and for watching episodes of *Father Knows Best* with me. I value her intelligent and witty commentary, especially on the various existential dilemmas of Betty Anderson. Amelie Hastie and Amy Lawrence showed enthusiasm for the project or writing process at the right moments, and I thank them. My husband, Mark Williams, always made me believe I was the right person to write a scholarly study of *Father Knows Best*. I thank him for not being annoyed at having to listen to the constant repetition of the program's theme music, which he dubbed the "a lesson is being learned" theme. Finally, I thank my late parents, Paul and Rosemary, and my brothers, Chris and Vincent, for their support. The book is dedicated to Vincent, who was my frequent after-school television-viewing companion. I hope he will find some of his favorite episodes discussed here.

*F*ather Knows Best (CBS 1954–1955; NBC 1955–1958; CBS 1958–1960) is one of the iconic television series of the 1950s. Like other programs of that era that are considered iconic, such as I Love Lucy and Leave It to Beaver, its status as such was established, and has been continuously reconfirmed, by its long history in rerun syndication and in its enduring fan base. However, the program is also remembered today via a cultural shorthand that views the 1950s as an era of massive conformity and authoritarianism, and this series, with its close-knit family looking to a wise "everyman father," as emblematic of those repressive social mechanisms. Yet, despite this dramatically contradictory status—recipient of both an enduring, positive response from longtime fans *and* condemnation or cynicism from today's critics who see the series as supporting the domestic containment logic of American ideology of the 1950s—*Father Knows Best* has received little in-depth or sustained critical attention from television scholars.

This book will navigate a critical space for examining the series that rejects monolithic positionings. I will use textual and extra-textual evidence to analyze the stylistic, generic, and industrial practices exemplified by *Father Knows Best* in relation to the social and cultural contexts in which the program was first produced and in which it has been received by audiences and critics for sixty years. My analysis will examine the social themes—such as change versus tradition, autonomy versus family togetherness, and self-fulfillment versus altruism—that animate the series, most of which are made explicit in the typically strong narrative closures of individual episodes. While the critics who have dismissed the series construe these themes, presumably reinforced by the episodes' "happy endings," as socially conservative, my argument is in line with television scholars, such as Horace Newcomb and Paul Hirsch (1994), who see audience engagement with the social values of television programs as related to how texts raise questions and open contradictions that cannot be reduced or dissolved by narrative closure. Blending melodrama and comedy, naturalistic acting and stylized cinematic visuals, *Father Knows Best* engages by making ideological tensions the very basis of its narrative problematics and by demonstrating that contemporary social contradictions are manifested, whether humorously or seriously, in the most typical of situations of the American family.

Adapted from a radio program of the same name (1949–1954) that was coproduced by Eugene B. Rodney and well-known film star Robert Young (who was also cast in the lead role), *Father Knows Best* is a television situation comedy focused on the everyday life of the Anderson family who live in the town of Springfield in an unnamed state. The characters include insurance-agent and family man James Anderson (Young), his wife, Margaret (Jane Wyatt), and their three children, teenagers Betty (Elinor Donahue) and Bud (Billy Gray), and the youngest child, Kathy (Lauren Chapin). Episode narratives typically end with the characters acquiring self-knowledge, often inspired or helped by their father, Jim. The series exemplified important generic trends in the era in which television became a mass medium. Specifically, *Father Knows Best* inherited the successful narrative formula for heartwarming family comedy from its own incarnation in radio and from its radio and television predecessors and contemporaries, such as *The Goldbergs* (middle-class Jewish family), *Mama* (turn-of-the-century immigrant Norwegian family in San Francisco), and *Make Room for Daddy* (urban, upper-middle-class entertainment family, some of whom are Lebanese-Americans), but embedded its family situations within the norms of contemporary middle-class, Anglo-American life in small town or suburban middle-America.

The indeterminacy of Springfield's status as locale is one of the successful ambiguities of the series. Many states in the union have a Springfield, and it is the capital of the heartland state of Illinois. In the program, Springfield is sometimes referred to as a small town with a pioneer history but is big enough to have a college and a television station. Because the program was shot in Columbia film studio's soundstages and back lots in southern California, the Andersons' home is visualized as part of a suburban tract neighborhood, which was characteristic of postwar California housing plans. However, the suburb was a real or fantasized locale of family living for many Americans, and, as interstate highways, shopping malls, and housing developments were constructed across the country throughout the 1950s, even some small towns started to resemble the upwardly mobile bedroom communities of the major cities that were the first suburbs. The type of setting represented in *Father Knows Best*'s Springfield—a town small enough that many people know one another but of a scale big enough to support middle-class neighborhoods and contain representative American business and educational institutions—would become paradigmatic for the family sitcom. The long-running parodic sitcom *The Simpsons* (1989–) named its small town/suburban setting Springfield some thirty years after *Father Knows Best* ended first-run production.

Although not the first program to be shot on film, *Father Knows Best* exemplifies the turn toward filmed programming in television of the mid-1950s and, in particular, filmed programming produced in California by Hollywood movie studios. *Father Knows Best* was a coproduction of Rodney-Young

The cast of *Father Knows Best*. (Rodney-Young Productions)

Productions and Screen Gems, a wholly owned subsidiary of Columbia Pictures. While it debuted three years into Screen Gems' production of telefilms, it was the studio's first situation comedy. Premiering in October 1954 in a Sunday 10:00 p.m. time slot on CBS, it was cancelled by its sponsor, Lorillard (owner of Kent cigarettes), at the end of the first season because its rating did not compensate for its high production expenses. Audience protest was so vehement that NBC picked the show up for its next season, airing it in a more family-friendly time slot, Wednesday nights at 8:30 p.m., with Scott Paper coming on as a sponsor and, later, the Lever Brothers buying in as an alternate sponsor. Ratings steadily increased over its six seasons, reaching number six in the Nielsen ratings during the 1959–1960 season, after which it ceased first-run production.

Ultimately, *Father Knows Best* was one of Screen Gems' most successful productions in network and off-network syndication.

It was broadcast in prime time on CBS and ABC for three years after first-run production ended, then aired on ABC daytime for five years before being made available for daytime off-network syndication, where it aired between the 1970s and the early 2000s on local broadcast stations, cable superstations, and niche-programming cable stations like The Family Channel and TV Land. The program was a groundbreaker in international television sales in both Europe and Asia, and, in 1957, it was the first wholly sponsored American network series to be sold to West Germany. By 2011, all six seasons were finally released on DVD, which included additional video materials such as behind-the-scenes production footage taken by Robert Young's wife, short documentaries featuring Elinor Donahue and Lauren Chapin, episodes of the Rodney-Young television series production that followed *Father Knows Best* (*Window on Main Street*, starring Young in 1960), and several audio recordings of the radio program episodes. The set also includes a short film, *Twenty-four Hours in Tyrantland*, which was commissioned by the U.S. Treasury Department about the value of U.S. Savings Bonds. Although the film featured the program's cast and characters, it was never broadcast on television but was instead made available for screenings in schools and community organizations.

Raucous variety-comedy programs, such as *The Milton Berle Show* or *The Colgate Comedy Hour* (with Jerry Lewis and Dean Martin), and the often surreal combination of situation comedy narrative and stand-up routines in such shows as *The Burns and Allen Show*, in which the performers (George Burns and Gracie Allen) played theatrical versions of themselves, are representative televisual comedy formats characteristic of the late 1940s and early 1950s. Many of these types of programs were still popular when *Father Knows Best* came on the air in 1954. But newspaper entertainment pages noted the flood of situation comedies that fall, with *Father Knows Best* often mentioned as a standout in the domestic comedy category (Wolters 1954). The program's radio predecessor had been praised for its ability to create comedy

5

plots out of the everyday events of a typical household rather than from joke-laden comedy routines; the television version of the program was seen as continuing this format but also exhibiting an emerging preference for naturalistic performance style and a generic blending of the comic with the melodramatic, producing what some would call a heartwarming effect. Although it may not have been immediately apparent, the generic and aesthetic trends that *Father Knows Best* exemplified represented the waning dominance of the physical, slapstick, self-consciously theatrical, and often comedian personality–based comedy, such as those mentioned above, that had been responsible for the mushrooming of television ownership in the first part of the decade. Laying the groundwork for programs that came on-air a few years later, such as *The Donna Reed Show* (1958–1966), also a Screen Gems–filmed series, and *Leave It to Beaver* (1957–1963), *Father Knows Best*, with its ensemble performance and story lines that always revealed the individual's imbrication within a familial context, was seen at the time, and continues to be seen, as epitomizing the central place held by family comedy-melodrama in prime-time television of the 1950s and early 1960s.

## The Domestic Situation Comedy: Social and Generic Contexts

Melodrama and comedy were established genres before the advent of television, of course, and had antecedents in theater, literature, film, and radio. While comic forms can be traced to ancient artistic practices, melodrama emerged as a genre or mode during the rise of the bourgeoisie and secular law as the basis for moral behavior. Early melodramatic narratives from the eighteenth and nineteenth centuries achieved closure by recognizing the moral innocence of protagonists who struggled under class or sexual oppression. According to Christine Gledhill, by the twentieth century, the form focused on the family, "with its ties of duty, love and conflict, the site where the individual is formed, and the center of bourgeois social arrangements" (Gledhill 1987, 31). In the period immediately following World War II, when *Father Knows Best* was broadcast on radio and then television, the role of the family in the individual's socialization as a bourgeois subject was scrutinized by many groups within American society, such as educators, religious leaders, and lawmakers. Diverse groups were united in "consensus" around economic and personal freedoms that were believed to characterize the American way of life as special and unique. But this was a way of life that some alleged relied on authoritative families' socialization of children through "containment" of rebellious energies that were believed to make America vulnerable to external forces that threatened those freedoms (Falk 2010; Medovoi 2005). While postwar film melodramas focused on families shared such long-established melodramatic aesthetic traditions as hyperbole, dramatic reversals, gestural and musical emphasis, and polarization between or within characters, they often registered the contradictions, conflicts, and pressures accompanying this socialization. Whether their narrative closures were secure and positive or open-ended and unable to contain the contradictions represented, cinematic domestic melodramas tended to be provocative and embraced serious subject matter.

The typical production and reception contexts for television broadcasts—commercial sponsors underwriting programs to be received within the family home—resulted in gentler, less controversial representations of the conflicts inherent in familial socialization than the film family melodramas (Liebman 1995). Some programs that were focused on families, such as *The Adventures of Ozzie and Harriet*, *The Aldrich Family*, and *The Life of Riley*, eschewed melodrama altogether and structured family conflicts entirely within comic terms. These situation comedies represented the family as a benevolent institution that was nevertheless subject to misunderstandings or miscalculations among its members. *The Goldbergs, Mama,* and *Father Knows Best* integrated their comedy with melodrama. These programs, like the more comic ones, structured narrative situations from, as well as found humor in, the everyday occurrences within the middle-class family. However, *The Goldbergs*, *Mama*, and *Father Knows Best* were also concerned with lessons about morality and emotional maturity. Everyday occurrences in *Father Knows Best* frequently develop into ethical crises for the children or their parents.

Episodes about fathers, sons, and newspaper routes in *The Adventures of Ozzie and Harriet* and *Father Knows Best* demonstrate the differing approaches and effects of these two kinds of "situation" or "domestic" comedies. In "The Boys' Paper Route" (Season 2), Harriet (Harriet Nelson) convinces husband Ozzie (Ozzie Nelson) to take their sons' paper route because she is worried that David (David Nelson) is coming down with a cold and that Ricky (Ricky Nelson) has not gotten enough sleep. The ensuing situation is played purely for laughs. Ozzie leaves with Harriet's address book rather than the newspaper subscription book; sleep-deprived, he struggles to deliver the papers in the rain. All ends well, as Harriet and the boys discover Ozzie's mistake and deliver the papers to the correct addresses; meanwhile, Ozzie's mistake results in new subscribers for the fledgling newspaper and greater exposure, through the paper's editorial, to the need for a new swimming pool for the neighborhood children.

In the *Father Knows Best* episode "Father Delivers the Papers" (Season 1), Bud has been doing a poor job of delivering newspapers. His boss threatens to fire him if he misses one more delivery. Jim and Margaret scold their son for his irresponsibility, but when Bud becomes ill, Jim takes his route so that Bud won't be fired. As in the *Ozzie and Harriet* episode, humor arises from the plight of a somewhat disgruntled middle-aged man delivering papers in the rain. Like Harriet, Margaret Anderson comes to her husband's aid, but *Father Knows Best* uses this plot development to represent Margaret's empathy for her husband's situation rather than an act of rectification of her husband's mistake. The crisis caused by Bud's bad performance at his job is averted, and Bud is shown, through the example of his parents' behavior, the way that mature people keep their commitments.

The situation that drives both episodes—fathers having to take over for their sons—is humorous because it is a reversal of the contemporary audience's expectations about generational roles and work: in the 1950s, it was expected that only boys would have the menial, low-paying job of newspaper delivery; yet it was also expected that a grown man could handle a job meant for a boy. Both Ozzie and Jim inspire laughter because their middle-aged bodies are clearly not up to the task of bicycling all over the neighborhood in an early morning rain. In the case of *Father Knows Best*, the lead character, Jim Anderson, is painfully aware of the humiliating aspects of his task, and although he sarcastically complains to his son and wife, he is also driven by the need to save his son from the boy's own irresponsible behavior. Bud is, at first, too immature to see his father's act as a sacrifice. The program is structured around not only humorous reversals in social expectations but also incongruities in the psychological understandings and ethical behaviors among characters of different generations and levels of emotional maturity. The incongruities are resolved in lessons: Bud is given a lesson in responsibility, and Jim recognizes how hard Bud's job really is as Jim encounters rude and demanding customers and the vulnerability of his own middle-aged body to such physical work. Both emerge from the experience more sympathetic to the other.

Paul Attallah's discussion of situation comedy in its "social comedy" form provides a helpful critical positioning of what I've described here, as his definition of this type of comedy suggests that the form is capacious enough to include meaningful cultural conflicts (Attallah 2003, 91–115). He points out that all genres have their specific ways of working out disequilibriums and disturbances to the social order. "Social comedy" (which can include family or domestic situation comedies) manifests disturbances in the equilibrium of socially institutionalized discursive hierarchies, such as those held by different generations, genders, or people of different social class or educational back-grounds. According to Attallah, humor arises from the clash between incongruous social beliefs and behaviors that are the result of these different discursive hierarchies. Situation come-dies focused on families almost always construct humor arising from the conflicting beliefs about the world held by parents and children, and/or those held by men and women, boys and girls. The narratives of *Father Knows Best* episodes often introduce these conflicts with characters making silly or sarcastic jokes, continue by developing the conflicts in a more melodramatic vein in which characters—through expressions of fear, anxiety, disappointment, etc.—register awareness of the serious per-sonal and social implications posed by the conflicts, and finally end or resolve the conflicts with a gentle, heartwarming humor that comes from the characters' better self-understanding and recommitment to the family unit.[1]

Audiences often remember *Father Knows Best* precisely for its "lessons." Critics have accused it of being an authoritarian text that naturalizes the middle-class family as the only way of being (Marc 1989; Spigel 1992; Liebman 1995). Yet the pro-gram's use of both melodramatic aesthetics and comic reversals reveals tensions in the status quo, raising questions that could hold as much weight as any solutions provided in its typically happy endings. Although *Father Knows Best* has plenty of epi-sodes devoted to the generational and gender conflicts endemic to most domestic situation comedies, its comedy is inclusive of other socially relevant concerns of its era, such as the meaning of success and the value of nonconformism. Ideological ten-sions or contradictions emerge out of this working-through of the disturbed social order as members of the Anderson family repeatedly encounter discursive hierarchies incompatible with those supporting their own way of thinking and living.

For example, in "Shoot for the Moon" (Season 3), a handy-man temporarily working for the Andersons refuses to take wages for his work, instead bartering work for a meal. He not only refutes the wage economy supporting the Andersons' lifestyle, but he also rejects the idea of having a permanent, material home in order to live in nature according to the Earth's cycles. Most significantly, he threatens the Andersons' parenting practices by demonstrating to Kathy (who wants to remove her warts) and Bud (who wants to win an essay contest) that the rational approaches suggested by their parents aren't necessarily solutions to their problems. The handyman performs a ritual ceremony that encourages the children by suggesting that they have the power within themselves to overcome their problems. When the handyman's nonmaterialistic, nature-aligned beliefs about an inner-directed strength are shown to be successful, the Andersons' material success and common sense assumptions about the superiority of their lifestyle—i.e., their ideology—which support their rational, "modern" parenting techniques and authority, are called into question. Yet, ultimately, Jim and

Sageman (Royal Dano) performs a ritual to teach the Andersons that they have power within themselves in "Shoot for the Moon."

Margaret Anderson prove to be open-minded (although Margaret takes longer to acquiesce to the handyman's philosophy than Jim does), and the episode's closure reaffirms the value of the family life exemplified by the Andersons. However disturbed their discursive social hierarchy is by the encounter with the Other or with what they have encountered within themselves, they don't repudiate their way of life. But they do, at least for the episode, experience insecurity about, and readjustment of, some of the assumptions that support aspects of their lives.

## Critical Dimensions of *Father Knows Best*

During the 1950s and early 1960s, *Father Knows Best* was considered by many social agents to be a television milestone. The program and cast members Robert Young and Jane Wyatt won many awards from religious, educational, and media organizations. It was also the first television program to be brought back on the air due to public outcry after its cancellation and the first to have reruns aired on networks in prime time after first-run production had ended. During that era, the program was so synonymous with the all-American family that the U.S. government requested the cast and characters for a film touting the importance of supporting national strength through the purchase of U.S. savings bonds. Today, the status of the series is poised between fan favoritism and, with few exceptions, critical opprobrium. My study of *Father Knows Best* is an attempt to contextualize the program, its popularity, and its critical position within its historical, industrial, and generic contexts, and to challenge oversimplified assumptions about its use of comedy and melodrama to explore the place of the family in mid-twentieth century American society.

Chapter 1 looks at *Father Knows Best* in its media industry and production contexts, including its origin on radio, its place within the history of Screen Gems telefilm production, and the backgrounds and creative philosophies of coproducer Eugene Rodney and star-producer Robert Young. The star persona and career trajectory of Young, who had a significant career in Hollywood films prior to his involvement with radio and television, provides a focus for much of this chapter, but I will also give attention to how Young and production partner Rodney considered the program's quality to be founded on bringing motion picture techniques, such as single-camera shooting, deep-focus photography, and effects lighting, to television. The visual style that resulted from Young and Rodney's choices had much to do with conveying the melodramatic values so important to the program's emotional impact.

Chapter 2 examines the social contexts for the creation and reception of *Father Knows Best*, especially in terms of the era's emphasis on family togetherness, shared parenting by both father and mother, and generational stages of the life cycle. The program's title suggests that paternal authority determines power hierarchies in the family; however, many episodes in the series present situations in which Jim is actually uncertain about the superiority of his knowledge. In addition, he frequently questions the meaning of professional and economic success. These insecurities about the status of paternal authority and the equation of masculinity with professional success and autonomy were characteristic of postwar class tensions and redefinitions of masculinity. A number of episodes will be examined in relation to these themes while others will be discussed in relation to the importance of family togetherness.

Chapter 3 will provide in-depth discussion of episodes that attend to the moral and social dilemmas emerging from conflicts and questions over appropriate gender roles for women. For some of the episodes, I examine multiple script versions accessed from the Eugene Rodney collection at UCLA to demonstrate how program writers struggled to represent contradictions in women's roles at the time. Some attention will also be given to how select episodes concerning Margaret's questioning of the value of her role as a housewife have similarities to episodes in other contemporary situation comedies, such as

*Mama* and *The Donna Reed Show*. These similarities suggest that the issue of women's experience of what Betty Friedan called "the feminine mystique" continually surfaced throughout the decade in what were considered innocuous mass cultural texts.

*Father Know Best*'s extensive rerun history and its current circulation via online sites and DVD sets are foundational to its presence in the public's popular memory of families and television in the 1950s; however, in the 1970s, producer Rodney and the series actors started to "rewrite" aspects of the program in television specials, talk show appearances, magazine and book interviews, and documentaries. Chapter 4 will discuss the ways that the cast participated in reevaluations of what the Anderson family meant in relation to "real families" of the 1950s, including their own. These reevaluations of the program from those involved in its production will be compared to how fans and scholars, many of whom grew up with the program, have used it to exemplify domestic containment ideologies of the 1950s and the ideological compromises of television as the most important mass medium of the mid-twentieth century. If many audiences negotiate the program in relation to the construction of a popular memory of what family life was like in the 1950s, popular historians as well as academic media scholars have often negotiated the program in relation to media theory and historiography since the 1970s that have critiqued mass media texts and institutions as complicit in oppressive social and cultural regimes.

*Father Knows Best*, like all mass media texts, reflects contradictions and conflicts of its historical moment and actively constructs responses to those tensions. Its continued circulation makes those contradictions and conflicts of the past available for reassessment in the present, and, in turn, those reassessments reveal the present's own social contradictions and conflicts. Over half a century since its first appearance, *Father Knows Best* continues to engage audiences—entertaining some and enraging others, but always providing a context for a culture to speak to itself about itself.

# Media Transitions, Media Legacies

Traditional series television is very formulaic, and situation comedy is perhaps the most rigid in structure and setting among prime-time programs. Opening credit sequences often introduce viewers to the setting and visualize the character relationships in montage sequences with the program's theme music as soundtrack. *Father Knows Best* had several different opening credit sequences in its six-year run, but all included images of the Andersons' house from exterior and/or interior views. In some versions, the first image is a long shot of the house's exterior followed by a cut to a medium shot of Jim Anderson leaving for his workday, sent off by his wife, Margaret, and gazed at by their children, Betty, Bud, and Kathy, who are standing on the stairway in the foyer near the front door, or, in one version, who come running up from outside to the half-open Dutch door of the kitchen. In another credit sequence, the first image is a medium shot of Jim returning home, welcomed by Margaret in the dining room as the children emerge from the kitchen to greet their father. In all versions, the swelling of the program's theme music and a male voice listing the cast

IN **FATHER KNOWS BEST**

Jim and Margaret kiss before Jim leaves for the office in one of the credit sequences for the program.

members are heard over the images. The first actual scenes of episode narratives often begin with Jim returning home, and he frequently announces his arrival to his family with a call into the living room or kitchen of, "Margaret, I'm home!" While not every episode started this way, it was a ubiquitous enough narrative opening that a short-lived 1991 situation comedy parody was titled *Hi Honey, I'm Home!*

The pairing of Robert Young as Jim Anderson with the Columbia studio set of the Anderson house in both opening credits and opening scenes is a significant redundancy, signaling the centrality of the father, Young as the star, and the home as a desirable and welcoming setting. Robert Young's star persona— that amalgam of on-screen and offscreen signifiers attributed to the actor—is one key to *Father Knows Best*'s production history and media intertextuality. Young's career trajectory, from

Hollywood studio contract player and film star to radio program star-producer to television program star-producer, represents the kinds of professional turns taken by many film performers in the postwar period when the motion picture studios began a state of decline and mass audiences turned more and more to broadcast media for entertainment. Unlike many of his contemporaries, Young's career across all these media had been supported by a publicity discourse emphasizing his private life as a devoted family man married to his childhood sweetheart and the father of four daughters.

This chapter will look at Young's career arc through the period of *Father Knows Best*, the origins of the program in Young's move to radio and how his portrayal of Jim Anderson and the tone of the program changed from the radio version to television, and his production partnership with Eugene Rodney, a former film producer who, like Young, favored bringing film production methods to *Father Knows Best* in its transition from radio to television. The way that Young appeared to comfortably and assuredly signify the typical American father was constructed from Young's experiences as a film and radio actor, the production partnerships and relations he had with producers and writers, and the publicity discourses and images that made connections between the private man and the characters he played.

## Robert Young: Consummate Actor, Family Man, Media Producer

A recurring anecdote in publicity about Robert Young and *Father Knows Best* goes something like this: one of Young's daughters asks him to help her with something, and when Young isn't able to solve the problem to her satisfaction, she laments, "But Jim Anderson always knows." Young would reply, "Well, Jim has excellent writers to solve all his problems!"[2] The story makes associations between Young and good fatherhood but also conveys that his character is a construct made up of lines written by scriptwriters and acted convincingly by a professional who is able to make viewers believe that Jim Anderson is a wise and caring father. Indeed, by the time *Father Knows Best* ended first-run production, the connection between the actor and Jim Anderson was so firm in the public's mind that Young had been honored many times by national parenting associations and was often approached by fans for advice on how to be a good father. Young felt highly ambivalent about the public's perception that he was just like Jim Anderson, as he would be later on in his career when fans wrote him for medical advice because they were convinced that he must be like Marcus Welby M.D., the general practitioner physician he played on the hit show of the same name (ABC 1969–1976).

However, *Father Knows Best* was a program that Young had sought out, helped create, and coproduced in a transitional moment in his acting career. He had been under contract at MGM Studios from 1931 until 1945. While he had success with a professional strategy of freelancing for several years in the late 1940s, radio series work, in which he had been participating since the 1930s—as a master of ceremonies for *Good News of 1938/ Maxwell House Coffee Time,* as a frequent guest performer on *Lux Radio Theatre*, *Screen Guild Theater*, and *Suspense*, and as a star of *Passport for Adams*—provided further opportunities to stretch himself as an actor in a variety of parts and offered a flexible work schedule when he had a concurrent film role.

*Father Knows Best* originated as a radio series in Young's desire for career diversification, but he was not its sole creative father. Young claimed that "no person created this show" ("Father Does Know Best" 1956, 9). Since radio's status as a source for stable work became questionable with the cancellation of *Passport for Adams* in 1947, he sought greater security with a series that would "fit the actor." With producing partner Eugene B. Rodney and writer Ed James, who had written gags for comedy sketches on the *Good News* program, they "sort of drifted into an idea for a family show that I would star in . . .

[since] I'm a pretty normal family man myself" ("Father Does Know Best" 1956, 9).

Young's status as a "normal family man" had been a key component of his on-screen and offscreen persona as a film actor/star, and although Young served as coproducer and co-owner of both radio and television versions of *Father Knows Best*, his well-honed skill in working with child actors and his public identification as a good father both on- and offscreen were his main contributions to the creation and maintenance of the program and its widely perceived sincerity. Young, born in 1907, had been signed at age twenty-four by MGM after a talent scout had spotted him onstage in a Pasadena Playhouse production. His first roles for the studio tended to be dutiful sons in melodramas or comedies. When Young was given romantic lead roles, these were usually in "programmers" meant to fit at either end of the double bill and budgeted somewhere between *A* and *B* quality. Young was often cast in them opposite such second-tier female stars as Florence Rice, Laraine Day, Ruth Hussey, or Ann Sothern. He was frequently loaned out to other studios, and when cast in *A* features, he was usually the second male lead who "lost the girl," be she played by such megastars as Joan Crawford, Margaret Sullavan, Claudette Colbert, or Greer Garson. He was in four films with Crawford, and his characters never ended up in the closing romantic clinch with the characters she played.

In an interview with Leonard Maltin in the 1980s, Young recounts that when he first arrived at MGM, studio production chief Louis B. Mayer felt that Young didn't have enough sex appeal (Maltin 2008, 13). Mayer advised the actor—not yet married to his high school sweetheart, Betty Henderson—to cultivate a playboy persona, complete with a bachelor apartment and servants who could help him host cocktail parties. He was told to be visible on the nightclub scene so that publicity could be constructed for him to suggest he was a "man about town." When Young found this to be a ludicrous charade,

MGM turned to a different publicity strategy, one that embraced Young's unassuming shyness and, after he married in 1933, included stories of his marriage, growing family, and sensible approach to his career. Consequently, fan magazine articles about him tended to have titles such as "They Asked Him to Kiss Joan Crawford and Robert Young Blushed!," "They Expect to Live Happily Ever After," "Young with Old Ideas," "Glamour is the Bunk," "Everything Under Control," "Girl Crazy [for his daughters]," "Career Man," and "How's Your Emotional Maturity?" Once his family grew, these articles almost always featured images of the actor with one or more of his daughters. By 1948, this publicity had congealed into observations such as the following: "[Young] is [a] solid family man with four daughters, a wife with whom he recently celebrated their fifteen wedding anniversary, and a house on a quiet residential street in Beverly Hills. . . . [This is] different . . . from the popular conception of a highly-paid, sought-after movie favorite's life" (Monroe 1948, 29). Fan magazines, which built up many stars as "glamorous" and even "mysterious," conveniently used the example of Young to demonstrate to any social reformer critical of show business or any fan resentful of star wealth that Hollywood performers are "normal" folks with aspirations for family and home, even living on "quiet residential street[s]."

Although Young grew frustrated with the roles offered to him by the studio, the possibilities afforded by the actor's growing "everyman" persona were not lost on MGM, and they occasionally cast him in quality parts that capitalized on his appeal. In *Northwest Passage* (1940), a high-budget, Technicolor film about Rogers' Rangers, the infamous military unit in the French and Indian War, he played second lead to Spencer Tracy's tough, heroic character, but Young's character is sympathetic and identifiable and the one for whom psychological growth, rather than heroism, is significant. Reportedly, director King Vidor had to fight the studio to cast Young in the leading role for *H. M. Pulham, Esq.* (1941) (Maltin 2008, 16). Vidor discerned that Young's "everyman" appeal was what was needed for a character who decides whether to live life according to his own desires or according to traditional expectations. Its gentle class satire and sincere approach to the life cycle of an ordinary man set a tone compatible with Young's low-key, naturalistic acting style and was an important developmental step in the actor's sense of what kind of characters he would favor in future productions.

Young also let other performers shine in their parts. These qualities came into play when MGM cast him in *Journey for Margaret* (1942) and *The Canterville Ghost* (1944) in which he costarred with child actress Margaret O'Brien. *Journey for Margaret* was based on the recent memoir of an American journalist in Europe during the first years of World War II. Assigned to a story covering an orphanage for children whose parents have been killed in the London Blitzkrieg, John Davis (Young) becomes emotionally attached to a young girl and boy; the film's story is mainly concerned with his difficulties in adopting them and finding a way to transport them back to the U.S.

War films, especially those produced by MGM, tended toward jingoism and sentimentality. *Journey for Margaret* certainly reaches for pathos and sentiment but refrains from political preaching, instead focusing on how war traumatizes young children. Much of its realism comes from Young's approach to the character as a man frustrated by his own powerlessness to help others suffering from the effects of war. Young enacts this frustration in small understated gestures rather than in overwrought expressions. Instead of the idolizing, courtly behavior that male stars often displayed toward characters played by child star Shirley Temple in her immensely successful films of the 1930s (including *Stowaway* in 1936, costarring Young as one of those adoring male protectors), Young plays Davis as amused and touched by Margaret (Margaret O'Brien) and Peter (William Severn) but cranky and impatient in his attempts to initially keep them at an emotional remove. The actor's interpretation of the character as a man learning how to balance professionalism and fatherhood is an important precursor to Jim Anderson of *Father Knows Best.* The heart of this film and *The Canterville Ghost* lies in the rapport between Young and O'Brien. The young actress was prone to wide-eyed expressions and a quivery line delivery, but Young's response was warm camaraderie rather than gushing reverence, tempering O'Brien's precociousness and keeping over-sentimentality at bay.

*The Canterville Ghost* was Young's last MGM film before he asked for a release from his contract, after which he started a nonexclusive contract with RKO, leaving him free to also pursue work of his own choosing. As a result, Young was in some of the strongest studio productions of the postwar period: as the bitter, disfigured flyer in *The Enchanted Cottage* (RKO, 1945); the responsible husband in *Claudia and David* (the 1946 sequel to *Claudia* [Twentieth-Century Fox, 1943]); the persistent police detective in *Crossfire* (RKO, 1947), a film noir about anti-Semitism; the philandering heel wrongly accused of murder in *They Won't Believe Me* (RKO, 1947); another character wrongly accused of murder in *Relentless* (1948), a western that Young coproduced with Eugene B. Rodney that was distributed by Columbia Pictures; and a harried father in *Sitting Pretty* (1948), a film from Twentieth Century-Fox that started a series of "Mr. Belvedere" movies with Clifton Webb. While these roles afforded Young opportunities to stretch as an actor, freelancing in Hollywood in the late 1940s and early 1950s was risky. Competition from television and the baby boom kept many adults at home, and theater attendance dropped. In addition, the studios were in transition mode after the 1948 Paramount divestment decree broke up their oligopolistic practices, divorcing them of their theater holdings.

The studios responded to these challenges by producing fewer films. While this climate favored independent productions, the competition among such production companies increased throughout the late 1940s and early 1950s; without long-term studio contracts, actors had to fight for each role, and less than successful films could not be financially propped up by a roster of successful ones by studios producing many at the same time. It is not surprising that consummate freelance actors like Young, who were not in the top ranks of stardom, would look to act in and produce series radio (and eventually series television) for security in this production climate.

## Rodney-Young Productions

Robert Young's association with Eugene B. Rodney, a former film publicist and producer, started when the actor was loaned out in 1935 by MGM to the low-budget production company Reliance, where Rodney served as an associate producer. They became close friends and formed Cavalier Productions (later Rodney-Young Productions) in 1947. Their main goal was to produce independent films starring Young, such as their western *Relentless*, released in 1948. But the company also became the producing entity for Young's ambitions in radio. While Rodney and Young were trying to find "a show that would fit the actor" who was a "normal family man," writer Ed James was eager to write a family comedy that would be distinguished from programs such as *The Life of Riley*, in which the father character was dim-witted and usually messed up his children's affairs (McLeod 2011, 2–3). In late 1948, Cavalier and James produced an audition tape of *Father Knows Best*. General Foods, parent company of Maxwell House Coffee and Post Bran Flakes, picked up the show as a sponsor in 1949. Starting in August of that year, *Father Knows Best* had a place on the NBC radio schedule for regular broadcast at 8:30 p.m. on Thursday nights.

Radio comedies focused on domestic life were already well established. *The Aldrich Family*, *The Life of Riley*, and *The Adventures of Ozzie and Harriet* created humor out of parent-child interaction; *Fibber McGee and Molly*, *The Bickersons*, and *Vic and Sade* found humor in the relationship between husbands and wives. Young claimed that *Father Knows Best* was different from the other family comedies because it had "a certain air of credibility about it" and a concern for showing "things that happen in the average happy American household" (Shanley 1956, 99; Talliaferro 1949). Some critics perceived the program in a similar vein. *The Chicago Daily Tribune* critic wrote in his review of the program about eighteen months after the program's debut:

> [T]he smiles arise from the recognition of the fact that the problems that harass Jim and Betty [sic] Anderson resemble countless crises of parents everywhere. . . . Don't look for any smashing punch lines. . . . The humor of *Father Knows Best* is gentle and lifelike. You have heard your own son and daughter come up with lines just as funny. Nor is the plot top heavy with strained, impossible situations often found in similar shows like *Life of Riley*, *The Aldrich Family*, and, of course, the soap operas (Reminah 1950, C7).

These observations not only support Young's view of the program but also imply that the program is situated between the family comedy and the melodrama while avoiding the implausibility of both those genres.

Evidence from *Father Knows Best* radio episodes suggests that Young and the newspaper reviewer's positioning of the program really describe the producers' aspirations, which were not fully achieved until the television incarnation. Radio episodes might have a quiet moment in which Jim alone, or in concert with wife Margaret, reflects on what they've learned as parents. This feature may have seemed to some at the time as a shift from the comic structures and goals of a program like *The Life of Riley*, which usually ended with the joke on the dumb father (who often spoke the episode's punch line phrase, "What a revoltin' development this is!"), but *Father Knows Best*, in its radio incarnation, is definitely heavier on laughs than emotional warmth. The pilot episode, for example, starts with Kathy whining to Margaret that she lost her skates, and within a few seconds we hear Jim crashing down the stairs as he slips on her misplaced skate. Kathy continues to whine at the breakfast table when Jim refuses to give her two dollars to buy angel's wings for a school costume. Bud comes in—after also looking for a misplaced item (his shoe)—and asks to use the family car. He begs and complains when his father refuses. Jim is happy, however, when Betty comes to the table and asks for nothing, but then she drops the bombshell that she and her boyfriend have decided to get married the following week. Jim goes from praising seventeen-year-old Betty for asking for nothing to exploding in shouts at her ridiculous announcement.

The scene exemplifies several established radio comedy principles. For example, situations that are not inherently funny (such as a child misplacing her skates) can be made so through an exaggerated vocal performance: it is Kathy's exaggerated whining, conveyed by the actress's voice, which is elevated in pitch and volume, that makes it funny (or annoying, depending on the listener). Sound effects are also a significant source of the humor—so the crashing sound that mimics a body falling on a hard, wooden staircase is funny to the degree to which it surprises listeners and makes us laugh at the body's contingency and vulnerability. The basis for the scene's central joke—that it is Betty, the last of the children to come to the table and the one with no request, who will end up disturbing Jim the most—is prolonged, structured by a principle known in comedy as "topping the joke." With the arrival of each child at the breakfast table, the problems escalate; Kathy's concern about her skates and wings is followed by Bud's begging to use the car, which is followed by Betty's announcement of her engagement. The "topping of the joke" comes not only from how long it takes for Betty to spring her news but also from dissonance between her nonchalant behavior in coming to the table—which leads Jim to believe at least one of his children is not going to ask for something inappropriate—and the content of her surprise announcement. This announcement, a kind of final breakfast-time revelation, causes Jim to practically spit out his coffee and ends up being the problem that structures the rest of the episode until its closure.

Betty's engagements, or her parents' fears that she will get engaged, are central to the plots of more than one radio and television episode. The television episodes treat the subject with some serious concern, but the radio episodes, as in this pilot, suggest that Betty is somewhat delusional. Jim, in particular, is sarcastic and otherwise hyperbolic in response to Betty's obvious interest in boys and marriage. Overall, Jim's behavior toward the children is much harsher and edgier in the radio incarnation of *Father Knows Best* than in the television version.

Jim is intelligent in the radio version of the program but also given to pontificating about some topic in a manner that the children, Margaret, or even Jim himself will end up contradicting or deflating by the end of the program. Apparently, Rodney and Young had initially thought that the program should be titled *Father Knows Best?* (Kisselhof 1995, 345).[3] The question mark was not approved by the sponsor and network, but the producers' effort in floating the idea suggests that they did not want Jim Anderson and paternal authority to be too idealized even if they rejected the "baggy-pants and red nose" that they associated with the "oaf" that William Bendix played on *The Life of Riley* (Shanley 1955, 1956; "Father Does Know Best" 1956).

Producer Eugene Rodney and writer and cocreator Ed James had a falling out, and it was intimated later in the press that it was over differences in approach to the characters and tone of the program (Eddy 1957). Although most critics who reviewed the program at its 1949 debut had perceived it to be in the "realistic" and "heartwarming" vein that Rodney and Young intended, two years into the program's run, R. L. Shayon wrote a scathing article in the *Saturday Review of Literature*, using an episode of *Father Knows Best* as an example of how fathers are often depicted as "jerks" or "fall guys" in popular media. This article may have prompted James's departure from the radio program around that time (Shayon 1951, 43). Roswell Rogers, who had been the head writer for the gentle folk-oriented program *Lum and Abner*, was hired to work with writer Paul West in 1952 to soften the edgy tone. West had experience writing for two other programs that featured dominant adult male characters interacting with child characters: *The Adventures of Ozzie and Harriet* and *The Great Gildersleeve*. He recalled later that "[*Father Knows Best*] was an entirely different show at the beginning. . . . I'd heard it a few times and I didn't like it. It was very quarrelsome, a lot of bickering" (Nachman 1998, 216).

One could argue with West's assessment that the program was "entirely different" before he and Rogers came on board the writing staff—although there might be less "bickering" in their scripts, the characters and types of situations changed little from the program's debut in 1949 to its end in early 1954. As we shall see, the real differences among *Father Knows Best* episodes emerge in the program's transition to television, and once on television, among episodes of different seasons, as melodrama is introduced and the children's characters (and the actors portraying them) grow older. However, publicity strategies for the radio version, and later the television version, remained in continuity with what MGM had created for Young—i.e., Young as a versatile actor and, more significantly, as the consummate family man with a soft heart for his wife and daughters. During the run of the radio program, magazines such as *Radio-TV Mirror*, *Parents Magazine*, and *Screenland*, as well as numerous newspaper articles, extolled the virtues and vulnerabilities of Robert Young's domestic skills. While articles with titles like "Father Knows Best," "We Have Four Daughters," "These Girls Know Father Best," and "Bringing Up Bob" admit that Young isn't quite as capable of solving every problem like Jim Anderson seems to be able to do, they also suggest that there is really not that much difference between actor and character in that both are focused on family and the emotional and moral growth of children in particular. Despite his frequent refrain that Jim Anderson was lucky to have writers to solve all his family problems, Young admitted to Walt Taliaferro of the *L.A. Daily News*, "Y'know, these situations [on the radio program] remind me so much of what goes on at home every day that I sometimes suspect this program is a documentary!" (Taliaferro 1949).

### *Father Knows Best* Transitions to Television

Minimizing the differences between Young and Anderson as fathers was not the only career challenge for Robert Young to weigh as the radio version of *Father Knows Best* aired into the early 1950s. The actor also had to decide whether to continue playing the part of Jim Anderson in a transition to television. By 1950, some of the most successful radio comedies—e.g., *The Goldbergs*, *The Aldrich Family*, *The Burns and Allen Show, The Jack Benny Show*—had started to make their appearance on television. By 1953, they had been joined by television versions of such radio domestic comedy stalwarts as *The Adventures of Ozzie and Harriet* and *The Life of Riley*. In addition, family situation comedies based on plays and/or films rather than radio programs, such as *Mama* and *Life with Father*, and newly created series just for television, such as *I Love Lucy*, *Make Room for Daddy*, and *The Stu Erwin Show*, were proving that television success with mass audiences did not depend only on the excitement brought by large musical spectaculars, anthology drama series, and the gag and stunt humor of physical comedians like Milton Berle and Jerry Lewis—all programming and performer types popular in the early years of television and heavily invested in by the networks.

Since Robert Young turned to radio in the late 1940s in part to find work security as he pursued the riskier film career as a freelance actor and co-owner of a production company, he had continued to act and look for film properties during the run of radio's *Father Knows Best*. In 1951, for instance, newspapers reported that the producing duo's company Cavalier Productions was preparing three films for Young to star in or direct. It was also reported that Young had asked *Father Knows Best* writer-creator Ed James to work on a motion picture treatment of the program. The latter project, turning the radio show into a feature film rather than making a transition directly to television, was not an unusual step. For example, Ozzie Nelson was filming a cinematic version of his radio series *The Adventures of Ozzie and Harriet* at this time, released in theaters as *Here Come the Nelsons* in February 1952, several months before the debut of the series on television as a regularly scheduled program. Actually, of the mentioned Cavalier Productions film projects, only *The Half-Breed*, a western released in 1952, came to fruition, and by that time, Rodney and Young had sold the property to RKO Studios. Yet, despite the success of so many domestic comedies on television and the failure of so many motion picture projects to get necessary financing, Young was reluctant to take his radio series to television: "when we had a chance to take it to TV, I thought it was a step down, a sign that you couldn't work anywhere else, but Gene [Rodney] convinced me otherwise" (Kisseloff 1995, 337).

Television in the early 1950s was in a highly volatile moment industrially and aesthetically. Young's attitude toward the medium is not surprising given that radio at the time was still attracting large audiences, and an actor could participate in it while still pursuing film or the stage. Television's overall career advantages for film actors or stars were not clearly defined. Articles in magazines and newspapers, as well as trade publications, debated the merits of television employing radio, stage, and film actors and stars for their programs, with some commentators suggesting that film stars would bring a glamour unsuitable to television's potential for intimacy with viewers while others claimed that film actors or star polish and glamour were needed in the fledgling medium.[4]

Perhaps most significantly, television was low on the hierarchies of what constituted cultural capital at this time. Telefilms—i.e., filmed programs made for television rather than live video broadcasts—had an especially bad reputation. The reputation was in some ways unfair, not so much earned as symptomatic of taste preferences based on cultural assumptions about what constituted "high," "low," and "middle-brow" cultures. As William Boddy and other scholars have shown, critics and even network executives often disparaged filmed programming in favor of live, spectacle-oriented broadcasts of comedy and musical variety programming featuring big stars or live anthology dramas starring Broadway actors (Boddy 1992).

The meaning of "live" and the history of "live broadcasts" are beyond the scope of this study, but the terms were often employed by critics to highlight what was unique about television (and before that, radio) in relation to film—i.e., that television could bring events and performances to audiences as they were happening. Spontaneity, timeliness, excitement, etc., were all seen as positive values of live television, making it comparable to theatrical performances and thus sharing in its high cultural capital. Some discourses suggested that live drama might be even better on television than onstage, as television could provide better views of the action for the viewer. Musical and comedy spectaculars, in which the host or guest stars built rapport with audiences by speaking or singing directly to viewers at home, were also praised for exploiting television's capacities as an electronic medium.

To some extent, the elevation of live television as "high" culture was partially an intra-industry competition as these programs tended to be produced in New York at network centers while telefilms were produced in Los Angeles and more than likely had an association with the film industry, which was making uneven but aggressive attempts to get in on television. Filmed programs offered possibilities for directors and actors to do retakes and for cinematographers and electricians to employ multiple camera and light setups—processes and effects associated with high-quality motion pictures—but the first telefilms tended to be shot within a couple of days and were too cheaply produced to exercise those advantages over live performance broadcasts. In other words, telefilms were associated with B movies, Los Angeles or Hollywood as a center of production, and qualities less specifically associated with electronic media's uniqueness, which, therefore, were believed by the networks to be less exploitable in drawing audiences to the set.

Screen Gems, a wholly owned subsidiary of Columbia Pictures studio headed by Ralph Cohn, was one of the Hollywood production companies of telefilms that contributed to the eventual dominance of film modes of production for series programming. Unlike some of the early telefilm companies, which tended to produce programming reminiscent of B movies not only in quality but also in terms of genre and content (crime thrillers, children's action programs), Screen Gems quickly became known for diversification in content and genre and in its approaches to production and distribution, which included coproduction partnerships with independent producers and personnel resources to pitch its programs to national sponsors and television networks or as syndication packages to network affiliates and/or local sponsors and independent channels (Anderson 1994). For independent producers who partnered with them, the advantages were numerous, including the use of its national sales force and studio production facilities and equipment. Screen Gems leased syndication rerun rights for network programs after they finished first-run production, and the independent producers usually retained ownership rights (as did Rodney-Young Productions).

Although detailed elaborations for Rodney-Young Production's decision to move *Father Knows Best* from radio to television are not included in primary sources I read for this study, it is likely that the aforementioned factors regarding Screen Gems were relevant to that decision. Screen Gems and other telefilm producers, such as Desilu and MCA's Revue Productions, had elevated the reputation of television productions made on film. By 1954, over 35 percent of programming on network affiliates was filmed material. But other factors may have come into play, especially for Young, who seems to have regarded television negatively in its early years. In 1951, when Rodney and Young were considering a version of *Father Knows Best* for theatrical exhibition, only about 23 percent of American households had televisions. By 1953, when the television program pilot was made (for screening on Screen Gems' *Ford Television Theatre*), 44 percent owned televisions. By 1954, when *Father Knows Best* was picked up by NBC and sponsor Lorillard, over 50 percent of American households had television sets. In addition, reruns, not possible with live broadcasts unless high-quality kinescopes were available, were emerging as another category of income for producers and coproducers of filmed programming. Clearly, television was a growing national medium and not necessarily a "last resort" for actors. Furthermore, debates about former film stars' incursions into television had peaked by the early 1950s. If there was still lingering animosity in some quarters toward the off-putting glamour of film stars on television, Young's everyman star persona was in tune with what many saw as the domestic qualities of warmth and friendliness that television could and, for many, *should*, bring into the home each week.

In its first year on the air, *Father Knows Best* cost about $32,000 an episode to produce. According to Screen Gems' Cohn, this was at the high end of the production scale for a half-hour telefilm. He designated $27,000 for an average filmed show and $22,000 for a low-cost thirty-minute program (Sinclair 1954). Actually, that same year, *The Adventures of Ozzie and Harriet* and *The Life of Riley,* at $34,000 an episode, and *I Love Lucy* and *Make Room for Daddy,* at $40,000, were more expensive half-hour programs. However, in comparison to productions that year of *December Bride* ($27,000), *The Stu Erwin Show* (aka *The Trouble with Father,* $28,000), *My Little Margie* ($30,000), and *I Married Joan* ($30,500), *Father Knows Best,* the newest situation comedy among this group, and Screen Gems, the newest telefilm company to enter into production of half-hour situation comedies, made a statement by starting at a cost in a higher range than these already established shows. While *Make Room for Daddy*, *Riley*, and *Lucy* were likely expensive due to salaries for their stars, the economic philosophy adhered to by Rodney-Young productions seemed to be all about creating and maintaining high-level story construction and performances and a high-quality visual look for the program.

Like many programs that made the transition from radio to television, the first and part of the second season of *Father Knows Best* relied heavily, though not exclusively, on scripts from the radio incarnation. As we shall see in the next chapter, most of these radio scripts were altered in significant ways to create a substantially different tone and emotional impact for the television program. The reworking of the radio scripts into multiple drafts of television scripts or "teleplays," both by the former radio scripters Rogers and West and newly hired writers, such as Dorothy Cooper, Sumner Long, and Phil Davis, suggested economic efficiency and the producers' painstaking efforts to make sure that the rhythm, tone, plot points, and characterizations of each episode were highly polished. In contemporary interviews as well as in vivid recollections later, members of the cast claimed that Rodney didn't let a script go into production unless he was satisfied with it and was so confidant in the excellence of the final draft that he wouldn't let actors "change one jot . . . [not] an 'and,' 'if,' or a 'but.' [Any changes] would take a call to the front office and Mr. Rodney would come down and discuss it with you" (Kisseloff, 342). Jane Wyatt was reluctant to join the cast when Rodney and Young contacted her for the part of Margaret Anderson because she preferred live television drama anthology series in New York, but "[she] fell in love with the script" they sent (Eddy 1957, 176).

Most of the program's production costs came from what were considered to be long rehearsal and shooting times. Cohn believed that two days of rehearsal and three days of shooting were needed for the half-hour filmed program, which was produced according to average costs. Each episode of *Father Knows Best*, on the other hand, took two days for rehearsal and three to six days for shooting. The set of *Father Knows Best*, constructed on a Columbia studio soundstage, was more elaborate than most sets for similar programs. The rooms were all made of three walls (mere one-wall backdrops were rarely if ever used, even in sets representing "outdoor" locales) although the sets representing the characters' bedrooms—regular but less frequent sites for story action than the living room and kitchen—had one or more removable walls that could quickly change the setting from one character's bedroom to another. The kitchen was fully functional, and so that the view from the kitchen window to the "outside" could actually reveal three-dimensional space, the kitchen door and window actually opened out to the set representing the patio and driveway.

Long rehearsals were not only needed for the actors to master the highly polished scripts but also for the more complex actor-camera blocking that was necessitated by the elaborate sets. Rodney and Young had decided to cast the main characters mostly with actors experienced in film, which meant that the practice of "hitting marks" (marks on the set floor to indicate to actors where they should be for correct lighting and camera range) was familiar to them. In addition to Young, actors Wyatt, Donahue, and Gray had extensive film acting experience. Only Lauren Chapin had no acting experience, and the producers chose her precisely for the potential naturalness that she could bring to a nine-year-old character.

Rodney and Young favored a visual look created from a variety of camera angles, a variety of shot distances and camera movements, deep-focus photography, and a range of lighting sources and effects—all of which required more shooting time.[5] Billy Gray, who portrayed Bud, recalled that "the kind of work that Rodney and Young did was so different from regular television. They didn't cut any corners at all. . . . The director . . . could have as many takes as he wanted to until he felt he got it right" (Kisseloff, 342). Young emphasized that it was an intentional strategy not just to use film for shooting but to shoot as if the program *were a film*: "[we] decided [it] would be shot like a motion picture. It would not be what was standard TV filming at the time, a two-shot over the shoulder, a close-up, and that's it. We wanted to give it some care and to indicate that we cared" (Kisseloff, 342).

Many of the episodes in the first two years were directed by motion picture director William D. Russell. During that same period, most of the cinematography was by either Frank G. Carson (aka "Kit Carson"), who had been a camera operator for many Columbia Pictures western feature films, or by William V. Skall, a veteran motion picture cinematographer who was an expert in Technicolor shooting and had served as the director

Robert Young and Jane Wyatt with veteran film and television director William D. Russell on the set of *Father Knows Best.* (Rodney-Young Productions)

of cinematography for Alfred Hitchcock's *Rope* and King Vidor's *Northwest Passage*, among other prestigious feature films.

Some critics who championed *Father Knows Best* when it was dropped by CBS in 1955 had reviewed the first episode of the program in October 1954. In their reviews, they used words like "realistic," "true-to-life," "credible," "believable," and "plausible" to describe aspects of the narrative structure and actors' performances. Jack Gould, a television critic for the *New York Times* who had not been a fan of the telefilm format when it first became apparent as a trend in early television, called the show "engagingly realistic" (Gould 1954, 35). *Broadcasting* magazine used some form of the word "real" (i.e., "reality," "realistic") five times in a single review ("In Review," 1954, 14). While none of the reviewers I sampled mentioned the deep-focus cinematography and the sets, Mary Beth Haralovich has argued that those qualities of the program contributed to the perception of its "realism" (1992). The detailed set representing the Andersons' home references recognizable—if somewhat idealized—contemporary domestic architecture, but many episodes suggest that the visualized spaces are also symbolic of the ideal of "home" and, in particular, the value of family togetherness dwelling within. The use of deep-focus photography, multiple camera setups, and often effects lighting (i.e., lighting that appears to come from natural sources in the room) are employed to emphasize the warmth and strength that comes from the family unit or the crises that threaten its cohesiveness and function as a site for moral growth.

These motion picture techniques differentiate *Father Knows Best* from other contemporary family situation comedies, even ones that were filmed, such as *The Life of Riley* and *The Stu Erwin Show*. Those two programs were either not conceptualized and/ or budgeted to use the time-consuming and costly techniques that produced the narratively and emotionally complex effects found in *Father Knows Best*. *The Life of Riley* and *The Stu Erwin Show* have cheap sets, resulting in vague spatial relationships among parts of the house, and sparse architectural or decorative details. Shallow-focused medium shots emphasize dialogue between two or three characters and physical shtick. Inserted close-ups and mismatches in eye-line gazes of the characters create disjointed shot/reverse-shot relationships. These shows visualize spaces that function as references to a *house* as a setting rather than fully realizing the space's realistic particularities or symbolizing these spaces as a *home* with all its connotations.

By contrast, *Father Knows Best* employs deep-focus photography and multiple camera distances and/or setups within a single scene to emphasize the importance of family togetherness within the home. For example, in the deep-focus shot midway through "Betty and the Jet Pilot," Jim and Margaret are in the living room in the foreground of the image as Betty opens the front door and walks into the foyer behind them. Jim is on the sofa reading the paper while Margaret is writing letters at the desk near him in the foreground of the composition, which is lit in a high key softened with a fill light appearing to come from the lamp at Margaret's desk. The scene suggests a relaxed, everyday scenario for the close-knit couple. Betty has been on a date with a jet pilot who is briefly stationed near Springfield; her entrance from the front door into the back space of the deep-focus composition can be read both literally and symbolically. Betty has been out of the house, exploring independence from her parents, but her continuing physical and emotional closeness to her parents is represented in her movement toward them from deep space and in the cut to a medium shot of the three, who are now turning their attention to each other as they gather around the sofa. Betty feels comfortable sharing her feelings about her new romance with the pilot even as looks of concern register on her parents' faces. Bud enters the frame from the dining room, and after a few seconds of dialogue there is a cut to a close-up of Betty and Bud as Betty indicates to Bud her greater understanding about romantic love. Margaret and Jim have not objected to Betty dating the pilot, but Betty's new

The mise-en-scène and cinematography of *Father Knows Best*, as exemplified in "Betty and the Jet Pilot," conveys the warmth of home.

emotional involvement threatens to change the family closeness that is now centralized in the visual composition of the shot. Ultimately, Betty and her pilot will put their romance on hold, as he is assigned to a faraway mission in Alaska. The nuclear family unit of the Andersons will remain intact. The desirableness of this particular family, as well the *ideal of family*, is communicated in the scene's carefully constructed visual construction to connote the home as a place for open communication and emotional closeness.

The employment of complex technological practices and visual stylization in *Father Knows Best* resulted in an affecting balance of realist denotation and symbolic connotation. The next two chapters will explore the tension among "realism," "melodrama," and "comedy" in *Father Knows Best* and how those modes of expression and generic categories shape what Father and Mother "know best" about in the program and for audiences of the 1950s.

# Fathers and Sons

In an unusual instance of self-reflexivity in *Father Knows Best*, the Season 2 episode "Father Is a Dope" opens with a shot of a television screen on which a (made-up) family situation comedy, *Father Does It Again,* is being broadcast. On-screen is George, the program's father character, who is trying to convince his wife, Hazel, that they will become rich from his plans to mine uranium. Hazel wearily nods her head at George's rantings, and each of their children parades into the kitchen announcing how they will have to give up their clothes or go to work now that all the family money will be going to their father's boondoggle. These laments prompt George to renounce his scheme and then laugh heartily when he realizes that his wife and children have organized their show of poverty to get him to drop his plans.

As the fictional program within the program comes to an end, there is a cut from the television screen to an image of the Anderson family. The camera pans across the faces of Margaret and the children, their eyes directed at the television before them. They chuckle at the antics of George and his television family; however, when the camera finally rests on Jim's face, he shakes his head with an expression of disgust and shuts off the television. Bud turns to him and asks, "How come mothers are always so much smarter than fathers?" The question sets Jim off on a lecture: "Only on television are . . . [fathers so stupid]— they've got poor old George so dumb so that he couldn't pour cider out of his boot if they had the instructions printed on the heel! He's so stupid that his wife doesn't dare tell him he's pulling another calamitous boner. No, she has to trick him, use the children as tools . . . they ought to change the title of that show from *Father Does It Again* to *Father Is a Dope*."

The fictional television program and Jim's diatribe against it are clear references to the types of contemporary father-centric television situation comedies, such as *The Life of Riley* and *The Trouble with Father* (aka *The Stu Erwin Show*), that critics had decried and from which Rodney, Young, and *Father Knows Best* writers so wanted to differentiate their father character and

The Season 2 episode "Father Is a Dope" includes a parody of family situation comedies.

Jim looks with skepticism at television's representation of fathers in
"Father Is a Dope."

suggests that what and how much Father knows is subject to
uncertainty or instability.

In the course of "Father Is a Dope," Jim evidences a belief that his family is conspiring together to play on his guilt
over how much he is needed by them so that he will abandon
his hunting trip with neighbor Ed Davis. He responds to their
every request with sarcasm. It turns out that Jim is wrong: Bud
does really need his help because he is sick, and Margaret really can't drive Kathy to a friend's birthday party because she
has to pick up a prescription for Bud. Jim then realizes that in
trying to prove that his family is just like the wife and children
schemers on *Father Does It Again*, he has only proven himself
to be as stupid as the program's character George. He drops his
plans and apologizes to Margaret. When she asks, "What for?"
he replies, "I hope you'll never have to know." Once he has left
to help the other children, Betty asks Margaret, "Don't you really know what he was apologizing for?" Margaret replies, "Of

course not," but then turns her gaze to the camera and winks, saying "It's amazing the ideas that some fathers pick up on that TV box!" Margaret's direct address to the viewer—a form of address that is rarely part of this series' aesthetic—leaves the issue of paternal stupidity and maternal scheming somewhat up in the air, even as it is admittance that television does influence what viewers think of families. Does Margaret's remark indicate that she was cleverly planning to keep Jim home or that she amusedly recognizes that Jim's recent sarcastic behavior toward the family was due to false assumptions that they were conspiring to keep him home?

Throughout the six-year run of *Father Knows Best*, the character of Jim Anderson is usually shown to "know best" or at least in ways equal to (if different from) his wife, Margaret, but often only after he has learned a lesson or two himself. Sometimes that lesson is that he has been arrogant enough to believe that he has all the answers. Lessons can be learned with humor or in seriousness—sometimes both. It is the structuring of narrative complications around lessons that ultimately result in moral and ethical self-knowledge that defines and differentiates *Father Knows Best* from the other family situation comedies that the episode "Father Is a Dope" is attempting to parody. How these lessons relate to the status of fathers and their epistemological authority, to parental power in general, and to the value of family togetherness is the program's particular way of negotiating changes in the genre and changes, tensions, and conflicts in the social context of its American postwar era.

## Does Father Know Best? Masculinity, Paternity, and the Postwar Family

Historians who have charted the shifting views and beliefs about masculinity and fatherhood in twentieth-century America stress the degree to which those identities were under stress and subject to instability, even though patriarchy itself, as a system of beliefs and behaviors and as a form of governance (i.e., institutionalized in laws informing the legal status of property), was the era's dominant ideology (Ehrenreich 1984; Weiss 2000). The postwar era of the late 1940s and 1950s—the period in which *Father Knows Best* thrived as a radio and then television program—is often considered to be characterized by a "normalization" of the nuclear family under paternal authority. While the trend away from extended families and the move to suburban enclaves, which further privatized and elevated nuclear family life, started as early as the nineteenth century, changes in the post–World War II period accelerated this process and sanctified the family as the main site for human growth and socialization. During this period, which was also known as the Cold War era (characterized by a cultural and contained military standoff between the "free world" of America and its allies and the communist Soviet Union and its allies), socialization of children was viewed as the primary goal of married couples. Strong morality, patriotic ideals, and confident self-image were believed to protect the American way of life from the "internal subversion" of communistic ideas and totalitarian rule. The building blocks for the individual's maturation within these inner strengths were to be modeled after upright parental behavior and authority.

The ideal citizen of the Cold War era was often pictured as the white, middle-class working man and father. Although this era was characterized by institutionalized sexism, homophobia, and racism—all of which enacted to elevate the white, middle-class male—legal challenges to institutionalized racism were in process in the 1950s, and goals for "tolerance" toward racial others and female aspirations were sometimes promoted by "liberal consensus" as signs of a positive and vigorous American democracy. As we shall see, these progressive goals exist in tentative or negotiated form in *Father Knows Best*, as was the case with much popular culture in the 1950s produced by dominant institutions aiming to capture a mass audience as well as corporate sponsors. Female aspirations, as will be discussed in the following chapter, do receive explicit attention in the program with some regularity, but week by week it is the status of Father's knowledge and the possibilities of family togetherness that are the program's main preoccupations.

The program frequently questions the meanings of American masculinity by asking, "What does Father know?" and "How does he learn from others?" These questions sometimes take the form of dramatic conflicts over the meaning of work, inheritance, generation, and how to temper male authority with caring parenting. Sociologist and historian Michael Kimmel has identified and given names to the ideals of American masculinity that have characterized politics since the colonial era as well as popular culture and sociology in the twentieth century (Kimmel 1996). Although his "genteel patriarch," an ideal of masculinity constructed on the basis of inherited wealth, land ownership, and aristocratic bearing, is not as relevant by the twentieth century, at least not for the middle-class male who is the focus of so many television representations, the "heroic artisan" and "self-made man" are worth exploring in relation to the character of Jim Anderson. Not only did *Father Knows Best* look back to the colonial era in several episodes (e.g., radio episode "Meaning of Freedom," television episodes "The Historical Andersons" and "Betty, the Pioneer Woman") to relate the Andersons to past traditions in American civic history, but the characteristics of masculinity that Kimmel identifies also have significant overlap with the powers and pressures of American manhood in postwar America.

The "heroic artisan" is a descendent of the "republican" citizen of the colonial era who was often an independent craftsman and shop owner. He is disciplined, responsible, and takes civic duty very seriously. His civic-mindedness and adherence to "producerism," or an economic autonomy coupled with a sense of political community, suggest that virtue comes in large part from hard work. The "self-made man" retains the "producerism" of the heroic artisan but is restless and anxious because success, which is won through aggressive competition, is often fleeting. The proving ground is the workplace, but this means always being watched and judged by other men; for this reason, manhood must be proved constantly. This last type of masculinity was analyzed in the era of *Father Knows Best* by various sociologists, including David Riesman, C. Wright Mills, and Erving Goffman. Riesman argues that the "inner-directed" man is autonomous because he acts out of an inner confidence rather than established norms. This type characterized the adventurous men who were foundational to the power of the national project in early America, and by the 1950s this type was severely challenged by pressures to conform and compete. The "outer-directed" man acts to please others and is best suited to the kind of professions exemplified by those who are salesmen or work for corporations. This is the corporate type identified by author Sloan Wilson as "the man in the grey flannel suit" in his novel of the same name, published in 1955, the year after *Father Knows Best* debuted on television.

Jim Anderson conforms to these stereotypes of masculinity in many ways: he is civic-minded, disciplined, hardworking, and, as the head of an insurance office in Springfield, he has some work autonomy. For example, he answers occasionally to a home office regarding general policy about the company, but he makes his own hours and all decisions about clients on a local level and speaks with a confident professional authority. He is willing to take risks at times and encourages his children to be adventurous in their aspirations. These qualities suggest that he shares aspects of the "heroic artisan" and the "inner-directed" man. But he also displays the anxieties of the "self-made" and "outer-directed" man; his very profession as a salesman puts him in the position of having to please others in order to make deals, and he sometimes worries about the judgment of other men over him or their professional superiority.

Jim even feels at times like he has lost his autonomy because of his job and the constrictions of suburban life.

Several episodes demonstrate how Jim Anderson, unlike Ozzie Nelson in *The Adventures of Ozzie and Harriet* (whose profession is left unclear) and Ward Cleaver in *Leave It to Beaver* (who is shown leaving and coming home from work but never at an office), is bedeviled by a number of workplace pressures. They also suggest that he shares many of the anxieties related to the pressures of postwar American masculinity as constructed within the previously discussed identity categories. In "Jim, the Farmer" (Season 1), Jim is convinced that he will be happier if he leaves the stresses of salesmanship to become a farmer. The episode opens with a shot in which Jim is constantly interrupted while dictating a letter to his secretary. While on the phone with an upset client, he takes a bottle of aspirin out of his desk drawer and swallows several tablets. When Lloyd, a junior associate, comes in, Jim jumps up to show him a photo of an apple farm that he wants to buy. He waves a disability insurance policy in his associate's face, claiming that a forty-nine year-old client is making a claim on it due to workplace stress. "I don't want this happening to me one day," laments Jim. He then offers to let Lloyd take over the insurance office. In the following scene at home, Jim clamors for Margaret's attention, telling her to quit hanging drapes, those "frivolous trapping[s] of materialism," because he needs to tell her that he's left the business to work "with his hands" instead of "letting a business run me."

Anticipating aspects of the counterculture by several years, Jim's plan is to get out from behind a desk and back to the earth, to feel free from the restrictions, responsibilities, and pressures of material goods that must be attained and maintained, and away from an office job in which he has to please others. Opening on a particularly stressful workday provides a convincing narrative setup for the series of events that follow—Jim's attempts to convince the family to move to a farm and his eventual hopes that his associate and secretary will call to say

Jim is ready to give up the stress of an office job in "Jim, the Farmer."

that he is still needed. Margaret privately informs Betty that her father has periodic urgings to leave his job, implying that Jim's dissatisfaction with his work is a recurring anxiety. Margaret believes that Jim's desires will pass, and she plans to get him back to the office.

The significance of the episode's closure is not that Margaret clandestinely asks Jim's colleagues to convince him that he is still needed (and he is, as the office is now falling apart in his absence) but that Jim learns a lesson about why his job as an insurance man is so important. It is the company's cleaning woman who teaches him the lesson. When Jim asks her if she ever tires of her job, she replies that she once wanted to be an actress, but she was terrible at it. Her father told her, "Don't try to be what you ain't. Find out what you are and be the best one at it." She is proud to be, at seventy-four, "the best [cleaning] girl in the building"; yet, her job doesn't give her the kinds of rewards that Jim receives, such as "the respect of folks in the community and the knowing that you are helping hundreds of people with their insurance at a time they need it." Her anecdote teaches Jim the "real" meaning of work. Even so, the episode glosses over the fact that while the cleaning woman may have a philosophy of work and service that convinces Jim to adopt her point of view, they become equals only on the basis of this newly shared philosophy of being the "best at what you are," not in terms of material compensation or respect in the community. The episode reflects tensions about labor within the social sphere and raises questions about the meaning of work and material success as a basis for modern masculine identity; however, the "heartwarming" lesson—while imparting an undeniable truth that doing something well and for others can be rewarding in nonmaterial ways—also reinstates the privilege of the middle-class white male who has a socially and materially rewarding job that will support a wife and three children and allow him to retire well before the age of seventy-four.

In "The Grass Is Greener" (Season 2), the social and personal value of attaining the successful "self-made man" ideal is explicitly addressed. Once again, the Andersons learn something about modern masculinity and the American dream of success from television. The episode opens as the Andersons watch a television talk show featuring one of Jim's college friends. Described by the program's host as one of America's "greatest industrial tycoons" and a "self-made man," Charlie Bradley has come to Springfield to open a steel plant. In the course of the interview, Bradley is asked about his college buddies with whom he was once known as one of the university's "four musketeers." One of the friends has become a foreign correspondent, another, a university president. When Bradley mentions Jim's name as the fourth "musketeer," the interviewer draws a blank and seems completely disinterested in the fact that the last friend in the group is only a local insurance salesman. Kathy has picked up on the social disparity between her father and his former friends, and, at dinner, she asks Jim why he isn't a success like the other "musketeers."

Kathy's unintentionally offensive question causes Jim to brood for the next several days. While the children's attempts to make their father feel better are played with gentle humor, Young portrays Jim as a man sliding into depression. For example, in the penultimate scene of the episode, when Jim comes home from work several days after Bradley's television appearance, Kathy's innocent question, and a series of encounters with a client who shows interest in Jim only because of his association with the "industrial tycoon," he plops down on one of the patio chairs, shoulders drooped, eyes staring vacantly. At moments he seems to be replaying the day's slights to his manhood as he shakes his head, grimaces, and wipes his hand across his mouth. Young's actions are underplayed and obvious at the same time. Each gesture is small and therefore perceived as naturalistic, but their cumulative power suggests that, in order to express Jim's distress, Young is using the performance codes of melodrama, in which psychic pain is displaced onto the body. Margaret finally alleviates some of Jim's suffering by telling him, in words reminiscent of the "lesson" of many episodes: "You're trying to measure success in terms of money. That's not always a yardstick. You're a success as a man, a husband and father. You're a credit to your community and to your family. What more could you possibly want?"

In the last scene, Charlie Bradley drops in after the Andersons' dinner. Kathy asks him, "If you can't bring your little girl with you [on your business trips], who fixes her roller skates when they are broken?" Again, one of Kathy's guileless questions prompts adult men to reassess the value of masculine success. As Bradley views Jim surrounded by his wife and children, Kathy sitting on her father's lap, he expresses envy of Jim's life, saying, "What's your secret, Jim? You seem so relaxed, so completely satisfied. You're not trying to beat your head against the wall as I am. I don't think I even know how to fix a roller skate."

While Kathy gets the last line in response to Bradley's melancholic admittance—"Then just ask my daddy; he can fix anything!"—the irony of Bradley's observation about Jim's "satisfaction" lingers in the scene's last image of Jim's rueful smile. Both Bradley and Jim are "successful" men who question the relation of that social value to their lives and its impact on their roles as fathers. Both "Jim, the Farmer" and "The Grass Is Greener" exemplify what Tasha G. Oren has described as the 1950s' situation comedy's renegotiation of "gendered labor divisions to allow for successful combination of work and parenting" for fathers (Oren 2003, 88). However, these episodes structure the renegotiation in terms of a questioning experienced as personal psychic pain that can only be expressed in the privacy of the family home and perhaps only alleviated there. Neither Jim nor Charlie Bradley easily expresses this pain at the office, and when Jim does so in "The Grass Is Greener," he is slightly hysterical until manipulated back to work by Margaret's ploy and the cleaning woman's lesson.

One of the assumptions regarding the relationship among duty, professional success, and manhood in the patriarchal systems of power is that a son will inherit, or perhaps surpass, his father's profession and social position. A number of episodes in the series are focused on the meaning of retirement in a man's life, on who will inherit Jim's insurance business, or on Jim's attempts to mentor young men in the profession. Both "Grandpa Retires" (Season 3) and "Time to Retire" (Season 6) concern older professionals who feel like "useless" old men when others decide it is time for them to retire. In the former episode, Margaret's mother has persuaded her husband to retire and sell his printing business to a younger man. Jim is brought in to adjudicate the transition, which has become difficult because Margaret's father is not cooperating with the prospective buyer. Jim ultimately arranges for his father-in-law to stay on the job training the interested, younger buyer and only retiring and selling when he is ready. In the latter episode, Jim is told by the home office that he must tell an older but subordinate associate, Mr. Higgins, that he must retire. Jim agrees with his family that the company-enforced retirement is unfair and agonizes about how to break the news. When Mr. Higgins finds out before Jim can discuss the matter with him, he runs off to his cabin in despair and humiliation. Bud, who is beginning to show an interest in working with his own father in business, finds Higgins and inspires him to fight for his right to continue working past the age when others think he is "useful." The two go back to the Anderson home and announce that Higgins will start his own company with Bud as his assistant. The episode ends with Jim—in the spirit of a professional who accepts competition—happy at this resolution and proud of his son's sensitive but assertive initiative in service to the older man. Both episodes raise issues about societal expectations for men's work, generational power, competition, and how pressures coming from economic and professional institutions quantify and shape expectations about men's "usefulness." However, the status of these pressures as problems systemic to patriarchal capitalism is displaced onto a personalized dynamic of older men versus younger men.

Jim's belief in Bud's potential for growth into a man capable of achieving professional, material, and familial success is usually rendered comically in the first few seasons of the series, when Bud is younger and immature. In "The Art of Salesmanship" (Season 2), for example, Jim is first excited when fourteen year-old Bud, who has become involved in a financial scheme to sell plastic gravy boats door-to-door, wants to try his hand at salesmanship. But Jim's enthusiasm is completely deflated when he witnesses how inept his son is at selling. He tries in vain to teach Bud the rudimentary gestures of sociability and authority that are needed to sell something to the skeptical housewives most likely answering their doors to his house call. Bud's attempts are comical and so is Jim's mounting frustration, which is mostly expressed in sarcastic jokes directed at the stupidity and naiveté of teenage boys. However, Jim starts to empathize with his son when he himself is unable to finish writing an entertainment routine that he promised for a community organization benefit. Through a lesson akin to the cleaning lady's "find out what you are and be the best at it" from the episode "Jim, the Farmer," Jim realizes that he has possibly not judged Bud fairly. He stops pushing Bud into a role for which he is unready or unsuited.

Numerous episodes concern Bud's immaturity and dubious judgment in matters of money, responsibility, or behavior toward his peers: "Live My Own Life," "Father Delivers the Papers," "Bud, the Ladykiller," "Bad Influence," "Carnival," "Bud, the Millionaire," "The Way of a Dictator," "Bud Quits School," "The Meanest Professor," and "Bud Plays It Safe." While Jim usually learns a lesson at the same time as his son, the prevalence of narrative problems motivated by the moral or psychological immaturity of the children demonstrates how much *Father Knows Best* was presuming a family audience for the program—one that included and flattered parents as well as entertained and taught children.

Mentorship of younger men and cycles of generational change are also themes that concern "The Promising Young Man" (Season 3) and "Turn the Other Cheek" (Season 6). In the former, Jim is asked by the home office's vice president to teach his son Woody how to be a good insurance salesman. Woody, much like Bud in "The Art of Salesmanship," is not a good pupil. But in Woody's case, his deficiencies in learning are a clear case of temperamental unsuitability and intellectual disinterest in the profession. Jim's efforts ultimately turn toward helping Woody's father understand his own son. In "Turn the Other Cheek," Jim befriends and gives advice to young Bart Holden who is just starting out as an insurance salesman. Bart tries to steal away a wealthy prospective client of Jim's using information that Jim has given him about this man. The family is frustrated that Jim won't retaliate against Bart. Having just advised Kathy that it is better "to turn the other cheek" rather than hurt a friend who has wronged her, Jim cannot bend his ethical stance. Ultimately, the wealthy client decides to sign with Jim because he trusts his slow, respectful, and ethical approach. Kathy learns from her father's example that revenge is never right or smart; however, Bart doesn't change his ways by the episode's closure. Many episodes of *Father Knows Best* demonstrate how Jim Anderson, as the ideal father and professional, or how the Anderson family, by their very example of moral courage, can lift up the ethical standards of the community. In this rare case, the program suggests that the example of one good man may be limited in its moral effects to the familial sphere.

Another set of episodes explores the relation of mature adult manhood to nonconformism. The concept of nonconformism has had a special place in American culture, dating back at least to the mid-nineteenth century philosophies of Ralph Waldo Emerson and Henry David Thoreau. By the postwar era, the concept had become resonant enough to echo in Robert Lindner's best-selling book titled *Must You Conform?*, in Riesman's idea of the "inner-directed man," as well as in the emerging literary Beat movement. "Betty Goes Steady" (Season 3), which will be discussed in the next chapter, "Shoot for the Moon" (Season 4), which was discussed in the Introduction, and "The Gold Turnip" (Season 5) focus on characters who test the boundaries of societal, peer group, and/or parental authority to elevate self-reliance in thought and nonconformity in action. Of the three, "The Gold Turnip" is centered specifically on father-son conflict over the merits of tradition versus nonconformism.

Bud's impending graduation from high school is the episode's central narrative event. Bud begs his father for a car for his graduation. Jim won't tell Bud what his present will be, but he is planning on giving Bud a watch that has been handed down by Anderson patriarchs to their sons for several generations. Unbeknownst to Jim, Bud has been deriding the traditions of graduation to Margaret. When he sees the watch on his father's dresser, he tells his mother he can't understand why this "old turnip" is so important to Jim. In a later scene, Bud pleads to the school graduation committee to abandon the idea of the traditional robe. Students and teachers on the committee contend that wearing robes is "the way it is always done." Bud takes on the robeless graduation as a crusade for nonconformism, one that gets him thrown out of the meeting and prompts the school principal to decree that only students wearing robes can march in the ceremony.

Jim and Margaret are disturbed and disappointed that Bud refuses to wear a robe. During an emotional encounter between Bud and his parents, Bud declares that he has to "stand [his] ground," that wearing robes at graduation is not what education is about, and that it is his record as a student that defines him rather than following tradition. Jim tells Bud that "they've taken about enough of this nonsense . . . [and that he has] to go to that graduation." Bud's response is a series of questions that demonstrate that the issue for him is a larger one than tradition: the issue is about the relation between individualism and manhood. "Why do you say I have to do it?" he asks. He continues, "Doesn't a guy ever reach an age where he has a say in what he does? Don't I have any right?" Bud runs up the stairs, but, hiding on the top of the landing, he listens to his parents talk to Mr. Messner, the father of his friend Claude. The parents share feelings of pride in their children and admit that the ceremony is validation of that pride, that it "is really for the parents." These words shift the ground of Bud's understanding of the ceremony's meaning. He now realizes that tradition can function to honor one's parents, and he agrees to wear the robe. When Jim ceremoniously gives Bud the watch, he quotes Polonius's speech in *Hamlet*, telling Bud, "to thine own self be true." He praises Bud for having the courage of his convictions but asks him to exercise them in places "where it counts a little more." In the last scene, Jim takes Bud to the garage to see the used car that the family has bought him for his graduation gift.

## Family Togetherness, Social Comedy, and Melodrama

In *Living Room Lectures: The Fifties Family in American Film and Television* (1995), Nina Liebman argues that the family situation comedies of this era can hardly be classified "as 'comedies,' so replete are they with anxiety, despair, and complication" (25). In this book's introduction, I used Paul Attallah's concept of "social comedy" to characterize *Father Knows Best* because this form of comedy makes humor out of the disturbances in the equilibrium of socially institutionalized discursive hierarchies. The basic operation of exposing ideological incongruities is also characteristic of melodrama, but instead of resulting in humor, melodramas involve their characters and audiences in "anxiety, despair, and complication." "The Gold Turnip," as many other episodes of *Father Knows Best*, alternates between the humor of "social comedy" and the anxiety and emotional complications of melodrama. Liebman tends to find the melodrama of these 1950s television series regressive and simplistic, especially in comparison to 1950s film family melodramas. Actually, despite the episode's trite symbolization of graduation robes and the happy ending in which Bud gets his wished-for car, the mise-en-scène that visualizes the conflicts is complexly rendered while the narrative and rhetorical orchestrations of conflict produce affect. These qualities facilitate questions about the larger social issues at stake—the values of nonconformism and the rights of children and young adults to differ from their parents' points of view.

The episode produces affect through melodramatic distantiation employed specifically in this example through construction of superior positions of knowledge for the viewer over the characters. In this way, the viewer understands the cross-purposed motivations and the web of complications that the characters find themselves in but cannot see. We know, for instance, that when Jim is wrapping the watch for Bud and telling Kathy that the gift will symbolizes Bud's attainment of manhood, Bud has already derided the watch as a symbol of worthless tradition. As a result, Jim's emotional vulnerability and later volatility is anticipated and felt by the viewer because we know at this moment what Jim does not. When Jim and Margaret feel disappointment and anger over Bud's refusal to wear the graduation robe, a refusal that will bar him from the ceremony, we know that they are ignorant of the courage that Bud displayed in making an argument to the graduation committee that each class should come up with their own ideas rather than blindingly following the traditions of others.

The mise-en-scène of the climatic confrontation between Jim and Bud is reminiscent of the melodramatic visualization of the confrontations between parents and children in film family melodramas, such as that between Jim Stark (James Dean) and his parents in *Rebel Without a Cause* (1954). Bud and Jim argue on the staircase, the liminal space between the public communal foyer and the living room spaces and the private spaces of the bedrooms upstairs, in which parents and each child have their own individually controlled domains. Bud is positioned higher on the stairs, slightly towering over Jim, symbolizing his belief in his idealistic superiority and the ascension of a new generation. In the shots in which Bud overhears his parents and Claude's father in the downstairs foyer, there is a cut from a close-up of Bud's face grimacing in anguish to a point of view shot in which we see, along with Bud, the parents below, who appear smaller, distant, and therefore vulnerable. The narrative and visual orchestrations of conflict have allowed the viewer to know about and feel for every character in ways that the characters cannot yet know about and feel for each other. The ending of the episode, in which Bud acknowledges and honors his parents' feelings and they recognize and honor the value of his

Against his father's wishes, Bud bucks tradition in "The Gold Turnip."

Jim gives Bud the Anderson pocket watch as Margaret, Betty, and Kathy look on in "The Gold Turnip."

fighting for convictions, produces the "heartwarming" ending that blends the closure of comedy with the emotional release of melodrama.

The emotionally fraught argument between Bud and Jim on the staircase of the family home is the closest that *Father Knows Best* gets in any episode to a generational shouting match. *Father Knows Best* employs melodramatic performance style (emphasizing exaggerated gestures and facial expressions and raised voices), visuals (mise-en-scène that positions characters and objects within symbolic configurations), and narrative construction of affect (the viewer's superior position to see and feel the cross-purposes and misunderstandings among characters) to demonstrate the worth of family togetherness rather than to explore the potentially bitter chasm of generational divide, which is often the subject of film family melodramas. In the world of *Father Knows Best*, family togetherness is always affirmed in the closure of each episode, but how to achieve and appreciate its value concerns many of its narratives. Often the possibility of family togetherness depends on Jim's demonstration that fathers assume the right balance among attentiveness, discipline, and emotional sensitivity.

According to sociologists and historians, the postwar male was supposed to temper whatever "male aggression" is needed for military success or the competitive workplace as well as soften the remoteness and sternness expected of patriarchs in the past in order to be the loving husband and father conducive to raising psychologically well-adjusted children (Ehrenreich 1983; Thomas 1988; Weiss 2000). While *Father Knows Best* never implies that Jim Anderson is or ever was an overly aggressive male, the historical evolution of these social ideals can be seen to some extent in changes to Jim's character from the radio to television versions of the program. The Season 1 television episode "Thanksgiving Day," which was adapted from a radio episode of the same name and basic plot, provides good examples of how Jim's sternness and arrogance was tempered in the media transition and how the television program adopted melodramatic characteristics to produce more emotionally effective situations and closures. In both episodes, Kathy has won a school contest for the best poem about Thanksgiving. Kathy's recitation of her poem is to be broadcast. Bud and Betty have accepted invitations for dinner elsewhere. In the radio version of the episode, as Jim and Margaret are home alone on Thanksgiving, listening to the radio broadcast of Kathy's poem, they reminisce about their childhood Thanksgivings. Kathy starts crying on-air and cannot finish her poem. The children come back home, and the family sits down to a Thanksgiving dinner of hamburgers, which, since she was counting on an empty nest that night, is all Margaret is prepared to serve. As they prepare to eat this humble dinner, Jim recites a prayer of thanks for all they have—most of all for "the gift of love for one another."

59

Kathy's poem, some of the dialogue about her poem, the children returning home, the hamburger dinner, and the exact

The Andersons gather around the kitchen table for their Thanksgiving hamburgers in "Thanksgiving Day." (Rodney-Young Productions)

wording of Jim's prayer make the transition from the radio to the television version. However, in the radio episode, which starts with Kathy reciting the poem to the family, Jim is impatient with Kathy's tentative reading and, insensitive to her nine-year-old sensibilities, belittles the poem to her face. Kathy has difficulty finding her place again in the poem each time her father interrupts her recitation but seems unfazed by the content of his remarks. When she reads the poem over the radio, Jim and Margaret feel sorry for Kathy's breakdown on-air, but their attitude change from sarcasm to sentimentality seems based on their own reminisces about childhood, not Kathy's upset. The return of Bud and Betty is not tied to Kathy's on-air performance. Until Jim's Thanksgiving grace, most of the dialogue and exaggerated vocal inflections (Kathy whines, Jim bellows) are geared toward laughs. The television version of the story, on the other hand, is constructed so that Jim has to connect his insensitivity to Kathy's breakdown while Bud and Betty return home because they have seen Kathy's breakdown on television and want to make their little sister feel loved.

The television episode sets up Jim for a lesson about his insensitivity with a new scene introducing the narrative complications. Jim receives a letter at the office announcing Kathy's poetry award. He rhapsodizes to the mailman and to his secretary, Miss Thomas, about Kathy's great talent, even comparing her to Elizabeth Barrett Browning and Shakespeare. While the viewer suspects that he exaggerates, the cut from this scene to an image of Kathy roughhousing in a football helmet at home makes that clear. The disparity between Jim's ideal of Kathy and the reality of her childish sensibility exposes Jim's unrealistic and unfair expectations about Kathy's ability as poet. At home that evening, Kathy is completely uninterested in her award, and it is Betty who reads the poem while Kathy runs out of the room to continue her playing. Jim's caustic insults at the quality of Kathy's poem are not said to her face, which, on the one hand, makes him a slightly kinder father than the character is in the radio incarnation. However, unbeknownst to the rest of the family, Kathy has overheard Jim's insults from her play space in the dining room. There is a cut from the parents in the living room to Kathy's tearstained face as she hears Jim's sarcastic commentary, and the result is pathos, not comedy. This situation motivates Kathy's breakdown on the air. Jim learns a lesson about his arrogance as he experiences Kathy's anguish. When Bud and Betty return home, they show kindness toward Kathy's hurt and embarrassment because they, too, have seen the broadcast.

At the end, the family gathers not in the formal dining room but around the smaller, more intimate kitchen table to eat their Thanksgiving hamburgers. Visual and narrative structures result in a tone that differentiates the television episode from the radio version and facilitates the viewer's experience of pathos and sentiment. The dinner is more than a holiday meal for the Andersons and the viewer: it symbolizes the rewards of family unity and affirms that caring and sensitive paternal behaviors are crucial to the desire for togetherness to become a reality. In episodes like "Thanksgiving Day," *Father Knows Best* seemed to respond to calls for the social and cultural elevation of the involved father, but the series also represents the roles of mothers and daughters as significant to the success of family togetherness. Chapter 3 will explore these roles as they relate to the era's conflicted social climate around domesticity and women's participation in labor outside the home.

# Women in the House

I f Jim Anderson is a representation of an ideal father, *Father Knows Best* suggests that a "father who knows best" is made of a combination of discipline, hard work, sensitivity, and a willingness to learn from others. Historical context demonstrates that this ideal is a social construct—contingent on shifts and conflicts in beliefs, experiences, economics, and political structures of postwar America—that elevates the father's place in both private and public spheres. The fact that Jim has to keep learning, across episodes, to temper his patriarchal powers with humility and love demonstrates that the ideal is not secure, that, in fact, the ideal is "new" rather than "natural." As discussed in Chapter 1, the program was developed as a vehicle for the actor-producer Young to combine challenging professional work with his personal experience of marriage and fatherhood. It is not surprising that this vehicle's narratives would privilege the head male role in a family. What is surprising, given the era's patriarchal assumptions that male public achievement was superior to "feminine" domesticity, as well as a contemporary critical discourse decrying how fathers were represented in family comedies, is how often *Father Knows Best* episodes sensitively explore women's roles as wives and mothers as well as the aspirations of daughters who frequently expect opportunities beyond the domestic sphere. Many years after the program's production, Elinor Donahue said of her character Betty, "she was so different than me . . . she knew where she was going." She was "ahead of [her] time," and tried to "get out there and not let gender be an issue" (Rothman 1988).

Donahue might have the privilege of hindsight in describing Betty as a "proto-feminist," but, by any measure, Betty is a formidable character. She is the best in her class, holds academic offices, pursues career options, and dreams of traveling as much as of marriage. Kathy, the youngest female in the Anderson household, is less powerful than her sister, but her life as a tomboy in the early years of the program allows the series during that time to explore aspects of childhood (e.g., belief in magic, taking care of wounded animals, jealousy of siblings) that are not gender specific. Margaret, as wife and mother, is shown to be as intelligent and sometimes as anguished as her husband, Jim. Like Jim, she is college-educated and civic-minded, and her work ethic is frequently held up as an example for the children. She doesn't drive the program's narratives as frequently as the other characters, but when Margaret becomes central to narrative action, it is through crises explicitly concerning the scope of her powers in the home and her desire to be respected as a homemaker as well as an intelligent, competent individual. In some cases, narrative crises around Margaret are about her relationships with women who have not followed her path as a housewife.

## Postwar Mothers and Domesticity

The postwar "involved" father emerged as a new social ideal for men through negotiations of the meanings of masculinity and family within a Cold War "consensus" public sphere (i.e., a heterogeneous public sphere unified around a commitment to anti-communism and by the rhetoric of liberal reform and expanded enfranchisement). Women's roles as wives and mothers were also in the process of negotiation in the postwar era. Historians have argued that "scientific" and "psychologically informed" parenting, which emphasized a stern but dispassionate mentality toward childrearing, displaced the concept of the "sentimental maternal" in the decades before World War II (Ehrenreich and English 1978; Coontz 1992; Plant 2010). In the "permissive" childrearing trend of the postwar period, parents were expected to be leaders but to treat children as expressive individuals rather than as a group that must be subjected to behavioral practices geared to make them "learn" when to be hungry or when not to cry.

However, the middle-class postwar mother was still subject to residual elements of the earlier ideals as she and the father of her children were now encouraged to be permissive parents. Left alone in nuclear family residences while their husbands worked at office jobs to meet the ideal of the successful professional and breadwinner, mothers were expected to be emotional caretakers as well as disciplinarians, consumers, and housekeepers. A widespread belief that communism could work through an "internal subversion" (i.e., through private life) was translated into, and compatible with, misogynist and homophobic messages that mothers could undermine American manhood through an over-attentiveness to their sons, making them "effeminate." Women were expected to prioritize home over career yet avoid "idleness" lest they become parasites on working men. This suggests that women walked a tightrope: being good consumers but not too idle; being a loving parent but not so indulgent and attentive that their children would remain psychologically dependent on them. Television historian Mary Beth Haralovich argues that women were expected to be satisfied with the "limited social subjectivity" offered them by the attention of consumer product industries and market researchers (128–38). However, even though *Father Knows Best* was developed to elevate the father over the "boob" characters of other contemporary television comedies and was praised by critics for restoring "dignity" to the paternal role, Margaret Anderson is depicted as a strong and intelligent individual.

Jane Wyatt, the actress who portrays Margaret, contributes to this characterization. Wyatt came from a socially prominent New York family that was descended on both sides from American "founding fathers." Her mother was a professional writer, and her sisters also pursued careers outside the home. Like Young, Wyatt had a well-publicized strong family life (at the time of her husband's death, they had been married for sixty-nine years) and an extensive background in film acting. She studied and worked with stage director Harold Clurman and stage and film actor-director Elia Kazan, both well-known leftist artists. She was active in Catholic charities and liberal causes and, like Young, joined the Committee for the First Amendment in 1947 to denounce the House Un-American Activities congressional hearings investigating communists and communist sympathizers within the film industry. Wyatt was blacklisted by the film and television industries for a brief time due to these earlier associations before appearing in *Father Knows Best*. Screen Gems required her to clear her name by reading an announcement on Radio Free Europe praising "American values."

Wyatt drew from this familial, social, political, and professional background in creating a personality and demeanor for Margaret that radiated intelligence and resolve. For instance, she often uses sarcasm to undercut her children's presumptuous attitudes, tells them when their expectations of her are unreasonable, and engages in playful verbal sparring with her husband, Jim, who treats her with respect. She occasionally disagrees with Jim's opinions on how to handle a situation with the children and is not afraid to tell him so. Although there are episodes in which Margaret indulges in stereotypical "feminine wiles" to get her way, these are rare. However, this generally positive and egalitarian representation of Margaret does not mean that the program creates a radically unconventional view of marriage and motherhood. In fact, episodes that focus on Margaret's "crises" are riddled with contradictions—many related to the social context discussed above—and there is evidence that the program's writers struggled to construct coherent and sympathetic situations and reactions for Margaret in episodes in which she compares herself to nondomestic women.

"Woman in the House" (Season 2) and "An Extraordinary Woman" (Season 5), two episodes in which Margaret compares herself to such female characters, are particularly telling of how the series struggles to negotiate ideas about traditional feminine gender roles with social, professional, and cultural alternatives for women. In "An Extraordinary Woman," the Andersons are visited by a former college friend of Jim and Margaret, Dr. Mary Lou Brown, now a doctor who has published a book about her fieldwork in African tribal communities. Dr. Brown and what she represents are catalysts for domestic tension even before her arrival. The night before Dr. Brown's visit, Jim reads passages of her book aloud to the family, and Margaret becomes agitated at his attention to Brown's achievements, believing herself to be "a born housewife." She later confides to Betty that she was rivals with Brown in college and always came in second place to her in school elections and sports. When Brown visits the Andersons, Margaret is ashamed that everything seems to be pointing toward her poor skills as a housewife: they are out of coffee, she hasn't finished cleaning the living room, the hot water heater that she thought she had fixed breaks down, etc. Finally, Margaret and Brown have a private conversation in which it is revealed that the doctor has always admired Margaret because she participated in competition for the experience, not for the "winning," and because Jim has told Dr. Brown that the way Margaret "goes about being a housewife and mother makes it an enviable art." Dr. Brown also reveals that she did lose something to Margaret—Jim. Margaret is able to be at peace with her feelings for Dr. Brown now that her roles as Jim's wife and as a

Marital discord between Margaret and Jim begins even before Dr. Brown arrives in "An Extraordinary Woman."

mother have been validated, knowing that she "has everything a woman could want."

The episode's resolution is representative of how the series often comes to narrative closure through affirmation of the value of conventional gender roles and the family. It is Margaret's "crisis" of confidence in her role that must be resolved. The crisis emerges out of Margaret's perception of the family's evaluation—especially Jim's evaluation—of Dr. Brown's achievements. However, even though it concludes with loving praise for the hard and socially significant work of homemakers over career women, the episode is structured around a positive appraisal of women's spirit of competitiveness and potential to achieve in careers, specifically in careers not traditional for women. When Bud implies that maybe Dr. Brown chose to work in Africa "because the hunting is better there," Jim disdainfully replies, "Bud, the woman who wrote this book is not trying to track down a prospective husband. . . . She is devoting her life to make people well," implying that women don't seek jobs as marriage markets. Yet, when Margaret expresses surprise that their friend has never married, Jim observes, "Oh, I don't know. . . . She was always a little too forceful for my tastes." After musing for a few seconds, he adds, "Of course, maybe that's why she has been so successful."

These exchanges exemplify how the program manifests *textual* contradictions as it works through the *social* contradictions of its era. Jim displays disgust with Bud's suggestion that Dr. Brown pursued an important profession as a way to get a husband—i.e., he recognizes and praises a woman's ability and desire for professional success apart from marriage goals— but, at the same time, he admits that her forcefulness mitigated his consideration of her as a potential mate. Historians have pointed out that while married women in this period were joining the workforce in record numbers, they were still expected to support their husbands' careers over their own and conform to domestic ideals and duties (Hartman 1994; Coontz 2005). When Margaret declares to Jim that she is impressed with Brown "because she is a woman, doing such a wonderful thing for humanity" and confides to Betty that she wishes she hadn't come in second best to Brown in achievements in school, the implication is that Margaret values nontraditional achievements for women and wishes that she could have been successful in this way, too. It is only after Dr. Brown tells Margaret how much Jim honors her homemaking skills that she finally feels reconciled with her choice to follow a traditional path.

Three different drafts of the script, written by Dorothy Cooper and revised at the suggestions of Rodney, suggest that the writer and producer struggled over how to portray Dr. Brown's achievements and the reactions of Margaret and Jim to them. Over the course of the script-drafting process, there is an increase in the number of Jim's positive assessments about Dr. Brown's achievements. In addition, Jim's criticism of Dr.

Dr. Brown (Constance Ford) tells Margaret that she envies her in
"An Extraordinary Woman."

Brown's forcefulness is softer and less clearly related to ideas
about conventional gender roles in the third draft than in the
second. In the earlier draft he says, "She was too, oh, forceful,
for *a woman*" [my emphasis] rather than "too forceful for my
tastes," as in the final version. His evaluation becomes more a
matter of his "taste" rather than a condemnation of successful
women. However, while Jim's dialogue emphasizes Dr. Brown's
courage in later versions, his opinions about Dr. Brown also
more directly contribute to Margaret's loss of self-confidence.
In the second draft, Margaret, not Jim, is the one who says,
"maybe that is why she has been so successful." Because Margaret has the line in this draft, the script gives her an opportunity
to have a meaningful self-reflection on women's typically limited opportunities, i.e., on how women who focus on a career
rather than marriage and family have opportunities for social
recognition that homemakers do not. When Jim is given the
line in the final version of the script, the implication is that

he, perhaps inadvertently, is putting homemakers down—i.e., professional women who are successful in helping humanity could not have done so if they had passively accepted the limited role of homemaker. The dramatic logic that follows from Jim's critical observation—one that will build to a crisis before the "happy ending"—is that Margaret loses confidence and will have to relearn that she is valued for being a wife and mother. This final version of the script demonstrates that Jim does indeed value homemakers as much as or more than courageous career women, but the implication is clear: professional success and homemaking success are probably mutually exclusive feminine achievements.

Evidence from drafts of the script for "Woman in the House" (Season 2) demonstrates even more pointedly how episodes depicting both domestic and nondomestic women were enmeshed in struggles and contradictions that required narratives to waver between inclusivity of possibilities for women and affirmation of the limited roles offered through conventional domestic ideals. In this episode, Jim's old friend Virge has moved to Springfield with his new bride, Jill, whom the Andersons have not met. When Virge and Jill come for dinner, the Andersons are shocked at Jill's unconventionality: she is probably twenty years younger than her husband (and Jim and Margaret), smokes, tries to engage in intellectual discussion about books, and makes insensitive jokes about the children and Margaret. The couple has not yet found a place to live, and Margaret is upset when Jim offers to let Jill stay with them for a few days when Virge is out of town. Margaret's resentment builds as she picks up after Jill; she feels like she is taking care of another child. In the climactic scene, Jill helps with Kathy by shampooing her hair while Margaret is cooking dinner. Recognizing that she is not wanted or respected by Margaret, and having admitted to Kathy that she has no friends or family other than her husband, she bursts into tears when Kathy asks if she can be her friend. Jill starts to prepare to move back to the hotel, but Margaret, having been told by Kathy of Jill's friendlessness, makes her feel wanted by asking her to participate in cooking the family dinner.

Jill is not just much younger than Margaret; her clothing, demeanor, and interests also suggest that she identifies with a cultural alternative to the middle-class domesticity of the Andersons and represented by the ladylike maturity of Margaret as a wife and mother. Jill first appears in an oversized pullover sweater, full skirt, neck scarf, and flat loafers. Her hair is not styled, and she smokes from a cigarette holder. Her expressions are affected and exaggerated. She makes references to psychoanalysis when she says Virge has a "daughter complex." When she asks Margaret if she has read Kafka, Margaret replies, "No, I don't even know who wrote it." Jill bursts out laughing, throwing her head back and slapping her knees. She further insults Margaret by pursuing literary references to Sartre and Baudelaire and by lobbing backhanded compliments at Margaret's homemaking efficiency. ("I'll bet she even makes her own clothes!" she shouts as Margaret leaves the living room for the kitchen.) Margaret tells Jim later that Jill made her feel like a stupid, "provincial housewife."

As in "An Extraordinary Woman," Margaret's understanding of homemaking and her competence at it are made strange or insecure to her in comparison to the achievements or judgments of another woman. In "Woman in the House," however, it is not in relation to a former rival of her own generation but a younger woman who asserts an intellectual superiority to distance herself from what Margaret offers in the way of well-versed social graces. For instance, Margaret is shown putting great care into her appearance and meal preparation prior to and during the guests' visit while Jill is dressed nonchalantly and admits to her own disinterest in housekeeping. The words "beat," "beatnik," and "rebel girl" are never used by any of the characters, but Jill's appearance and her investment in existential literature and psychological complexes, as well as low-brow culture (when Jill first arrives, she tries to find wrestling shows on their television), suggest that

Jill (Mary Webster) displays her knowledge of literature to Margaret in "Woman in the House."

she fits into those categories even if her marriage to a middle-aged peer of Jim and Margaret does not.

Young women who identified with the Beat movement were attracted to this movement by its rejection of middle-class domesticity, despite the fact that many of the male beats who inspired them were motivated by sexism as much as by class critique (Breines 1994; Medovoi 2005). Rebellious young women demonstrated their rejections of normative femininity through displays of cultural capital—as in Jill's claim to know the works of Kafka and Sartre—and a sartorial style that studiously avoided suggestions of conventionalized feminine delicacy. One social fear about such women was that these kinds of displays signified an uncontrolled sexuality. It is likely that *Father Knows Best* would have had problems with the network's Standards and Practices Department (which monitored representations considered not suitable for a family audience) if Jill had been portrayed as overly sexual, but changes across multiple drafts of the script demonstrate that writer Roswell Rogers originally conceived of the character as a very flirtatious woman who irritated Margaret as much by her sexual demonstrativeness as by her irresponsibility and rejection of dominant norms of femininity.

In the first draft of the script, Jill engages in flirtatious banter and behavior with a cabdriver, the mailman, and Jim. Jim pleads with Margaret to accept Jill by observing, "She is really a very lonely person," to which Margaret responds, "Oh? She's made friends with every male within a radius of twelve miles." Margaret even makes such remarks directly to Jill: when Jill says that she misses her husband, Margaret snidely says, "I thought we had a big enough variety of men around here to keep a girl from getting lonesome." Margaret is so suspicious of Jill's motives regarding men in this version of the script that her turnaround and acceptance of

Jill at the end doesn't seem dramatically motivated. The second version of the script, which is very close to the final shooting script, drops almost all of the scenes and allusions to Jill's flirtatiousness as well as Margaret's suspicion that Jill is oversexed. Jill's remark about Virge having a "daughter complex" toward her is added to the scene of the couple's initial visit, and this becomes the episode's reigning analysis of Jill's character: she is childlike and insecure, not an overly sexualized young woman who hates what Margaret symbolizes of normative femininity. The drama will lead to Margaret learning this truth about Jill. The second draft also adds the scene in which Jill shampoos Kathy's hair; this action—and Kathy's revelation to Margaret that Jill lacks friends—provides dramatic motivation for Margaret's change in feelings.

"Woman in the House" manages to mitigate the threat of the "rebel girl" to the social order by desexualizing the type, defining her as emotionally and socially immature, and making her happiness hinge on participating in domestic duties. At the same time, in the revised conclusion, Margaret does realize that she has been unfairly punishing Jill as an irresponsible and disrespectful daughter rather than treating her as a mature woman who could be a friend. In addition, the final image of the episode can be read as a reflection on the smugness of narrative resolutions that disavow the contradictions raised by the text: while Jill is helping Betty and Jim with the dishes, Margaret lies on the living room sofa reading Kafka's *The Trial*.

This concluding image appeared in the very first version of the script. In that version, Margaret tries to explain the novel's premise to Jim: "[T]his is a wonderful book. It is all about a man who is arrested, but doesn't know why." Even though the accompanying line of dialogue is dropped in the final version, the remaining image retains much of the idea conveyed by the first draft's dialogue—namely, the fear of being judged that informs Jill's insecurity about what she has done to upset Margaret and Margaret's ignorance about the real motivations behind Jill's behavior. The image of Margaret's obvious enjoyment of a novel critiquing authoritarianism also undercuts aspects of Margaret's "lesson" with irony—namely, the irony that despite the "happy" resolution to their conflicts, the women have shared, through their experiences with one another (and the novel), the burden of fulfilling gender role expectations as well as feelings of entrapment and alienation.

Jane Wyatt complained to Rodney that the first season's scripts gave her little to do with Margaret's character (Wyatt, *Archive of American Television*). Rodney promised that this would change. Not only did Margaret have a bigger role in most of the episodes from Seasons 2–6, but there were at least two episodes per season focused specifically on Margaret's crises over her roles as a wife and mother. The value of women's emotional and physical caretaking and the family's lack of acknowledgment of, or participation in, these labors motivate a variety of episodes of *Father Knows Best*, such as "Margaret Disowns Her Family," "A Medal for Margaret," "Close Decision," "Dilemma for Margaret," "Brief Holiday," "Margaret's Other Family," "It's a Small World," and "Good Joke on Mom." The fear of Kafkaesque entrapment expressed in "Woman in the House" lingers on in "Brief Holiday" (Season 5). In this episode, Margaret

Margaret reads Kafka at the conclusion of "Woman in the House."

finds herself identifying with Kathy's caged frog, which Kathy expects Margaret to care for while she is at school. As the episode opens, Margaret is washing dishes, and the children and Jim are leaving for the day. Betty leaves a dress for Margaret to alter, Bud expects her to press his corduroy trousers, and Jim wants her to call a repairman. After they have all left, Margaret literally throws in the dish towel and decides to escape for the day to Orleans Street, a part of town that looks like "little Europe," with outdoor cafes, market stalls, and strolling artists. She treats herself to a new hat and lunch. As she chats with an artist who sketches her, she tells him of her fantasy of an "unfettered life." Then she dashes off hurriedly when she realizes that it is time for the children to be returning home from school.

To this point in the story, the episode presents a fairly conventional and sympathetic act of a woman who wants to temporarily escape from too many obligations that she performs to the underappreciation of others. It is the depiction of Margaret's return home that sharpens the critique of how women are robbed of authority through traditional gender role expectations. As Margaret resumes washing dishes, the children enter the kitchen one at a time, and each expresses surprise at her apparently underwhelming housekeeping: "What happened to you today?" "What'd you do, goof off all day?" "Shouldn't you be cooking by now?" Margaret answers each with sarcasm but finally bursts out in anger when Jim asks, "Aren't you behind schedule today?" She accuses of him of spying on her. He backs off but starts to interrogate her again after the Orleans Street artist drops by to give Margaret the sketch that she forgot when she rushed away. Jim refuses to believe Margaret's confession that she "just felt like leaving" for the day. Again, he drops the matter, but at the office the next day, he gazes at the sketch of Margaret, and we hear his thoughts in a voice-over: "Who are you? You're not Margaret. . . . How did we become strangers to one another?"

In fact, what has become strange is Jim's normalization of "housewife" or "homemaker," at least as these terms relate to the wife he believes would not "flit off on a whim." He poses the story of Margaret's disappearance in the guise of a "hypothetical" to his secretary, Miss Thomas, who replies that this woman "is evidently seeking an escape from something." Afraid that Margaret will leave him, Jim rushes home and overhears her comparing herself to Kathy's caged frog. After Margaret tells Jim that her greatest distress is his refusal to believe that she left just to get away from housework, he apologizes and starts to lecture the children about their unfair expectations that their mother will do their work. The final image is of Margaret and Jim enjoying a dinner on Orleans Street.

The value of women's housekeeping labor and the degree to which those duties defined wives and mothers as housewives is the subject of episodes of other family comedies during this era. "Mama's Bad Day," an episode of *Mama,* follows the title character through a day of typical housekeeping, registering her anxieties, resentments, and guilt about her family's expectations of her role as a homemaker. The "Just a Housewife" episode of *The Donna Reed Show* cleverly examines the social and familial attitudes that have made "just a housewife" a demeaning phrase. Joanne Morreale examines this and other episodes of *The Donna Reed Show* that focus on the tensions of women's roles in the postwar family to argue that the series regularly spotlighted the social values of women's work and female authority. However, even contemporary reviewers made an issue of Margaret's work as a domestic laborer in *Father Knows Best*. In "Is Robert Young Fair to Jane Wyatt?" *Variety* columnist Mannie Manheim declares that Margaret is the hardest-working mother on television, noting that each time he sees her character she is "caring for a large bundle of wet-wash, ironing, or shelling peas" (Manheim 1960, 99). Meant as a humorous meditation on the paucity of representations of housework in many television shows, the *Variety* piece observes that perhaps Margaret seems overworked because Harriet Nelson of *Ozzie and Harriet* never seems to have "housework problems" while many other programs dispense with the problem of representing wives performing domestic labor by creating servant characters to take care of housework.

## Betty Anderson: Reproduction of Gender Roles or Rebellion?

Manheim notes that Margaret often has her teenage daughter, Betty, help with kitchen work. Although familial expectations for children's household labor had decreased by the 1950s, children were often assigned chores. Girls in particular were expected to help with domestic duties that would carry over into their adult lives as wives and mothers. The Andersons have this expectation for Betty. In fact, when Jim takes Margaret out to dinner at the end of "Brief Holiday," he snaps at Betty to "make dinner for the other children." Some aspects of Betty's characterization in the series are very conventional: she is a full participant in adolescent social rituals of dances and parties, overly concerned with appearance, and often jealous of other girls her age if they have more boyfriends or have achieved more than she has. However, next to Jim's character, Betty's changed the most from the radio to the television version of the program. Whereas on radio she was initially written as boy crazy and constantly threatening elopement or early marriage, Betty in the television series is popular with boys and even falls in love but is never shown as desperate to marry. (In Season 5, she decides not to marry her longtime boyfriend.) The radio version of Betty is often stupid and naïve, but the television version of Betty is the smartest, most confident, and, usually, the most honored girl in school. Betty on the television program also takes on social causes and, in more than one episode, sets out to prove that she can do something as well as or better than a boy.

In "The Gold Turnip," Bud demonstrates a rebellious nonconformity, but his character is usually portrayed as easygoing or even likely to capitulate to peer pressure. Among the Anderson children, Betty is the one most likely to fight for her convictions, and the program shapes some of her dilemmas explicitly as existential crises in "The Bus to Nowhere," for instance, in which she questions the meaning of life and runs away from home; and in "The Homing Pigeon," in which she envisions her home as a prison and begs her family to let her move into an apartment with an older girlfriend. "Betty Goes Steady" (Season 3) most directly confronts the values of nonconformity that created identity crises for Jim and Bud in other episodes. As was the case with Bud's nonconformist stance over graduation robes, the pretext for Betty's adoption of nonconformity might seem trite: Betty learns that the social system at her college is conformist and elitist when she realizes that only certain clothes, hangouts, and dating rituals are considered to be "acceptable" to her peers. Yet, such social systems are not insignificant, as they are central to maintaining and bolstering gender and class distinctions among young people as they try out adulthood in the liminal space of college. The episode emboldens Betty to eventually critique her peers for their judgments and rejection of "social unacceptables" but shows its own cautious hand in casting the teacher of Betty's lesson as a (slightly) older man. The male character is Mr. Beekman, Bud's high school journalism advisor, who is taking classes at Betty's college. When he comes over to the Andersons' house to help Bud lay out the front page of the high school newspaper, he and Betty argue over the merits of the college social system. Betty makes the point that since social conventions frown on women going "stag" (attending a dance solo) or taking the social initiative with men, other systems, like "going steady" (dating one person exclusively), can provide women compensation by securing their entry into mixed-gender situations; however, Beekman's argument about the conformist and judgmental elitism of the system is shown to be correct—almost every attitude, canned expression, appearance, and code of the "acceptables" that Beekman has identified to Betty is apparent when her own socially "acceptable" steady shows up on the doorstep for a date.

The use of a male character to convey the message of nonconformity—which he does through arguments supported by quotations from Emerson and Thoreau—legitimizes the young woman's adoption of the philosophy. From our present-day perspective, depicting a male character as Betty's intellectual superior seems condescending, but like the "rebel girl" who adopted the codes of the male Beats in the 1950s, Betty finds that a male role model easily inspires her own stirrings toward independent thinking. However, although Betty's attitudinal change is shown to be difficult for her, the lesson is taught and learned with much more humor than melodrama as Mr. Beekman and Betty engage in clever wordplay disagreements in a variety of encounters. Like romantic comedy films, "Betty Goes Steady" presents verbal sparring between men and women as a pleasurable fantasy situation in which women are granted equality with men through their displays of intelligence and wit.

"Betty, Girl Engineer" (Season 2) also uses aspects of romantic comedy's characterizations and narrative in exploring Betty's attempt to find a vocation. She chooses—against the wishes of her high school guidance counselor and the advice of her parents—to do a weeklong internship with an engineering and surveying crew. On the job, she is subjected to what today is called sexual harassment. She quits but is vocal about her male supervisor's sexist judgments. Doyle Hobbs, her supervisor, shows up at the Andersons' home to ask Betty for a date. Betty overhears him telling Jim that Betty could make "a darn good engineer" but that would be a "trick" on men who deserve to find a homemaker waiting for them after work, someone "like [their] mother." Betty agrees to go out with Hobbs, even though she never renounces her interest in engineering.

The barbs between Betty and Hobbs are pointed and funny, and they conform to the "meet cute" banter that characterizes romantic comedies and leads to the eventual détente and union. Hobbs is invested in the idea that Betty should conform to a gender role whose main function seems to be supporting male achievement. Betty's parents sympathize with her disappointment, yet Margaret seems happy when Betty finally shows interest in a dress she has bought her to mark her "growing up," i.e, leaving girlhood for womanhood. The character reactions to Betty's choices suggest that the episode is working through the vicissitudes of the reproduction of gender roles, i.e., the pedagogical and behavioral practices employed to direct young people into normative gender roles. Although Betty never renounces her interest in engineering (only Hobbs's attitudes toward that interest), the narrative closure seems weighted to present Betty's gendered normalization as the "happy ending"; however, evidence from previous drafts of the script suggest that the episode scriptwriter and/or producer engaged in a negotiation of various attitudes about traditional versus alternative roles for women on the way to this resolution. The episode's opening scene depicts a male high school guidance counselor signing up Betty and her classmates for their vocational internships. Male students choose a variety of career possibilities, and the counselor enthusiastically signs them up for appropriate internships; however, he tells each female student to sign her name next to the box labeled "secretarial work." Betty astonishes the counselor and the other male students by her refusal to accept their idea of women's work and is adamant about choosing the box labeled "engineering." This scene did not appear in earlier drafts of the episode. Its later inclusion provides a strong context for the viewer to judge the subsequent masculine attitudes toward Betty as unfairly limiting. The episode's author, Roswell Rogers, claimed later that Betty's abrupt turn-around at closure didn't "ring true" to him; he felt forced into an unmotivated ending by the strictures of the twenty-six-minute teleplay format (Liebman, 49). These script changes provide evidence that the function of the added opening scene with the guidance counselor is to negotiate the conflict between careers and heteronormative femininity by making it difficult to read the romantic conclusion as an unmitigated happy ending. In other words, Doyle Hobbs's attitudes are revealed as yet another way that men pressure women into traditional roles. Indeed, barriers to Betty's desire to take up nontraditional roles resurfaced throughout the run of the series as "problems" for her to negotiate, if not always conquer.

In "Betty, Pioneer Woman" (Season 5), Betty's belief in women's equality as a principle and support from other women as an experience are important motivating factors in her drive for achievement. Betty has been put in charge of the Chamber of Commerce's Springfield Founder's Day project, which will consist of a reenactment of the trek that town founder, Jonas Wentworth, made to Springfield with his wife, Agatha. Betty has decided to cast college classmate Tom, a great-grandson of

Betty verbally spars with engineer Doyle Hobbs (Roger Smith) in "Betty, Girl Engineer."

the Wentworths, in the role of Jonas. After a series of nasty exchanges with Tom, during which he praises the courage of his great-grandmother but accuses modern girls of being "too coddled" to make the trek, Betty takes on the cause of women's equality. However, she can't find a female classmate to make the trek, so she decides to do it herself. Meanwhile, Tom has been quoted in the town newspaper deriding modern women's abilities. A reporter tells Betty that the "honor and glory of the women in Springfield" relies on her success as Agatha in the reenactment. Betty starts receiving telegrams, supplies, and good luck charms from women in Springfield in support of her cause. During the trek, Springfield residents gather in the town square with an announcer who reports the couple's whereabouts via radio telecommunications at points along the twelve-mile trek. Springfield men echo Tom's misogynist beliefs while their wives comment sarcastically on male hubris. When

Betty has more strength and fortitude than her male partner
in "Betty, Pioneer Woman."

Betty and Tom finally arrive in the town square, Betty is pulling the cart for Tom, who has sprained his ankle and has to
rest inside. She proves to everyone that modern women are as
brave and capable as men. A few days later, Tom brings Betty a
cookbook owned by his great-grandmother Agatha, telling her
that he will eat a piece of "humble pie."

As with the episodes discussed earlier that focused on Betty,
the narrative of "Betty, Pioneer Woman" is structured as both a
battle of the sexes and a battle of ideas about gender as expressed
through the dueling wits of Betty and her male rival. Tom tells
Betty that modern girls only know how to "cook a frozen dinner" while man is "still the hunter, the warrior." Betty rejoins,
"I've never heard such rubbish in my entire life. . . . You have
a bump of male superiority as high as a camel's back. . . . your
sophomoric ideas [are] nothing but an idiotic echo from the dark
ages!" Crosscutting is used in this scene to alternate between

the sparring couple and Margaret, who is preparing cookies in the kitchen. Margaret's face registers annoyance every time Tom speaks, and, later, when she offers him a cookie, she icily says, "If anyone wants to know, these cookies are homemade."

The episode exemplifies the program's tendency to portray Betty as ambitious to prove that she is strong enough to overcome traditional attitudes about women. What distinguishes "Betty, Pioneer Woman" from other episodes with similar themes is the demonstrable support of Margaret and other women toward Betty's ambitions and the fact that Betty "wins" her argument with Tom without qualifications. Some episodes, such as "Betty Makes a Choice," "Betty's Career Problem," "Betty Finds a Cause," and "Big Sister," position Betty's drive to win as a selfish obsession. In "Big Sister" (Season 4), Betty is the top counselor at the summer camp that Kathy attends, but Betty is unrelenting in prodding her sister to be the star camper—to the point that she is ruining Kathy's self-confidence. Bud tells Betty that Betty wants Kathy to win not for Kathy's sake but for her own glory. Earlier in the episode, Margaret had approvingly accepted Betty's competitive spirit by observing "that's the way you're made," but Bud's judgment that Betty's hyper-driven ideals of achievement are often selfish turns out to be correct.

*Father Knows Best* recognizes that the role of women at home and what it means to be successful *and* a woman is in flux: Betty is a pioneer woman in more ways than one as she constantly challenges herself and those around her to rethink their assumptions about gender roles, even as she enthusiastically throws herself into dating rituals and beauty regimens that conform to normative femininity. However, the program was clearly struggling to negotiate positions for Margaret and Betty that are characterized by a joint appreciation of domesticity and public achievement, which historian Joanne Meyerowitz argues was the endorsed perspective of much popular journalism in the 1950s (Meyerowitz 1994). Not only were its notions of gender enmeshed in social contradictions of the time, but the episodic, rather than serialized, structure of the narratives and the multi-authored scripts meant that the program varied from week to week in attitude toward the "woman problem." Yet, across the series' duration, we see not only Margaret's discontents but also her increasing support of Betty's goals. Where she was once so concerned in Season 2's "Betty, Girl Engineer" that Betty conform to socially acceptable feminine roles, by Seasons 5 and 6 she is more likely to support how Betty is broadening public conception of what constitutes women's roles. These roles are part of the discursive dynamic in later consideration of the program by the cast, fans, and critics.

# Rerun and Rewritten

I n its last year of first-run production, *Father Knows Best* aired several episodes that self-consciously reflect on the significance of the Andersons to the ideal American family. In "Family Contest," an episode that particularly stands out in its reflections about families, the Andersons enter a contest for a Hawaiian vacation awarded to the family whose photo portrait best exemplifies the ideal American family. Kathy fears that the family of their neighborhood baker, Henry Henslee (Stu Erwin), will win the contest. Henry's family includes the very photogenic Toby, a Korean War orphan adopted by the family after the eldest Henslee son died in battle. Kathy tears up the photo of the Henslees taken by Betty and hides the negative so that they will miss the contest deadline. After Kathy meets Toby, who offers friendship and expresses his excitement about Hawaii, she feels so guilty that she retrieves the negative, confiding in Betty about her misdeed so that Betty can develop another photo and submit it for the Henslees by the deadline. In the episode's final scene, the Andersons gather around the kitchen table to look

Kathy hopes that a photo of her family will win the Andersons a trip to Hawaii in "Family Contest."

at a photo of the Henslees enjoying their win in Hawaii as the ideal American family.

This episode demonstrates the degree to which the program's producers and writers felt compelled to acknowledge and explore the critical and audience elevation of the Andersons as the representative American family, even going so far as to cast Stu Erwin, the actor who played one of the bumbling television fathers against which *Father Knows Best* defined itself, as the head of the Henslee clan. By this time, the series had won awards from the television industry and religious and civic organizations. It had not only steadily climbed in viewership ratings, breaking the top ten in this sixth and last season, but also had surpassed other popular family situation comedies—*The Adventures of Ozzie and Harriet, Leave It to Beaver,* and *The Donna Reed Show*—which did not or only rarely made it into the top twenty-five rated programs during the years they overlapped on the air with *Father Knows Best*. Earlier chapters have explored how the program was part of a wave of family comedies, like *The Adventures of Ozzie and Harriet*, and comedy-melodramas, like *The Goldbergs* and *Mama*, which were broadcast on radio and/or television in the 1950s. Its blend of comedy and melodrama, focus on "lessons," middle-class suburban setting, claims to representativeness, and visual style influenced programs that came on the air later in the 1950s or early 1960s, such as *The Donna Reed Show*, *Leave It to Beaver*, and *My Three Sons*. *The Cosby Show* of the 1980s–1990s, which also focused on an involved father and intelligent mother of several children and presented moral lessons, has been identified as a later progeny of *Father Knows Best* while series such as *Married with Children* (1987–1997), *The Simpsons* (1989–present), and *Family Guy* (1999–present) are said to be anti-*Father Knows Best* programs (Frazer and Frazer 1993).

*Father Knows Best* was unique in many ways among comparative programs of the 1950s: the program's status as an "answer" to contemporary debates about radio and television representations of fathers, its sensitive explorations of masculine and feminine roles, the particular changes it made in transition from radio program to television series, its "resurrection" by fans and critics after its first season cancellation, its reruns aired on prime-time network hours for three years after it ended production, its civic awards unprecedented for a situation comedy, etc. All these elements unique to *Father Knows Best* have tended to be forgotten when, over a period of fifty or sixty years, it has been shown and discussed along with all of the era's other family situation comedies that have been rerun in syndication during that time.

Nostalgic and camp notions of "classic TV" as well as elite notions of "television heritage" emerging from journalistic and scholarly accounts of 1950s' situation comedy's relation to Cold War America have tended to lump these shows together.[6] While their use of generic formulas, an overlapping pool of creative talent (e.g., writers and/or directors of episodes of *Father Knows Best* also wrote and/or directed some episodes of *The Donna Reed Show*, *Leave It to Beaver*, and *My Three Sons*), and shared historical contexts suggest that critics should discuss these programs in relation to one another, many have tended to do so for the purposes of wholesale dismissal of them based on their representational exclusions of nonwhite, working-class characters and explicit social problems, elisions that are considered proof of their complicity with "reactionary" political forces of the decade in which they were produced and first made popular with mass audiences. While it is beyond the scope of this study to rewrite the history of the 1950s, television criticism in relation to that decade, or the role of the rerun to the continuing popularity of 1950s' situation comedies, the legacy of *Father Knows Best* is bound up with these contextual categories. The ways established analyses of the program have articulated or elided these interrelations suggests what is at stake in considering the place of *Father Knows Best* as a "TV Milestone."

## From Reruns to Popular Reassessments

Television scholar Derek Kompare argues that reruns "represent not so much a dormant past as a dynamic *television heritage*: . . . [a] body of series, genres, stars . . . which culturally anchor the past few decades in the contemporary public memory." The history of how and when a program is rerun "sets parameters for the ways in which the past is discursively activated" (Kompare 2002, 20–21). Repeats of *Father Knows Best* episodes first aired in prime time on CBS and ABC for three years following the end of the program's production and airing of first-run episodes at the end of the 1959–1960 television season. Throughout the 1960s and early 1970s, the series was rerun in daytime hours, first on ABC and then off-network. Cable television's The Family Channel—the 1990 re-titled and re-branded Christian Broadcasting Network channel—aired two episodes per day in the early 1990s. Later in the 1990s and early 2000s, the program had a spotty presence on Viacom's Nick at Nite as well as on the channel's spin-off, TV Land, which was created when Nick at Nite phased out reruns of early television programs on its schedule. At the time of this writing, the program can be seen on the broadcast and cable channel MeTV, online on Hulu and YouTube, and is available for purchase on DVD. In this prolonged period in reruns, the series has been re-experienced, or experienced for the first time, by audiences no longer contemporaneous with the social, cultural, and industrial forces characterizing the era in which the program was first broadcast. The episode repeats entered into a dynamic relation with the concerns of the audience's present—i.e., reruns made the white middle-class Anderson family of the 1950s continuously available to be read against changes in the ideals and realities of family life, race and class relations, and mass media forms of later periods. Reading *Father Knows Best* through its afterlife in reruns has affected public memory or understanding of the 1950s, as well as the role television played in the 1950s. These effects can be seen in fan responses, journalistic accounts, editorials and academic scholarship, and in the reflections and professional activities of those involved in the production of the series.

## *Father Knows Best Reunion; or, The Andersons Grow Up*

The continued popularity of *Father Knows Best* in reruns into the 1970s inspired two made-for-television movies, *Father Knows Best Reunion* (1977) and *Home for Christmas* (1977), that reunited the cast of the original series. Although set in the late 1970s, these television movies were representative of a collective reconsideration of 1950s' familial values as seen through that era's television programming. Both incorporate "flashback" footage from 1950s' *Father Knows Best* episodes to serve as reminders of the importance of family togetherness for the characters at the time of the movies' filming. In each movie, the children have returned to the family home at turning points in their personal relationships: Betty, a department store buyer, is a widow and mother who has to decide whether to rekindle her romance with the jet pilot of Season 3 of the series; Bud, the owner of a motorcycle gear shop and a racer, is in a troubled marital relationship because he is too often away from home; Kathy, an unmarried teacher, is trying to decide whether to marry a widower with two sons. The narratives noticeably avoid what was, by the 1970s, the reality of divorce as the show emphasizes the enduring marital bond of the Anderson parents and uses the grown children's experiences with absent or dead spouses as a way to negotiate the era's trend toward multiple or delayed marriages. Betty and Kathy are career women, like many white middle-class women of the 1970s, but have been married and/or are contemplating marriage—assurance that public achievement will be combined with domesticity in the age of the women's movement.

To publicize the broadcasts of the television movies, the cast was interviewed for newspaper articles and on television talk shows. In these venues, they reflected on the cultural, social, and personal meanings of *Father Knows Best* in the 1950s and in their present moment. Audiences and journalists have continued, as of the writing of this book, to be receptive to the cast's reflections on *Father Knows Best* as circulated in memoirs, oral histories, newspaper and television interviews, documentaries, and even obituaries. (Young died in 1998, Wyatt in 2006.) In many of these texts of the last forty-five years, the dynamic between journalist/ interviewer and cast member/ interviewee is characterized by contestation over such concepts as realism and idealization, the role of television as a mass medium, the role of television genres in relation to social reality, and what constitutes family.

For example, an article in the *New York Times* coinciding with the airing of the first television movie reunion conjures up a fantastic popular memory of both the 1950s and the series' representational strategies through its hyperbolic recollections of Margaret "whipping up Norman Rockwell suppers" and Betty "all aflutter over her boyfriends," even as it admits that the Andersons were an "idealized American family" (Eskenazi 1977). The article's main emphasis is on the "reality" of the lives of the actors who played Betty, Bud, and Kathy at the time of the series as contrasted with the characters they played and the people they are now. It recounts the stories of the teenage Lauren Chapin suing her alcoholic mother for her program salary, Billy Gray's 1960 arrest for marijuana possession during the period in which the program was in prime-time network reruns, and Elinor Donahue's teenage marriage and divorce during the production of the program. It is mentioned that none of the child actors had a father at home, but, according to the article, they are happy and productive adults in 1977 due partially to the inspiration of, or relationships forged on, *Father Knows Best*. A *Los Angeles Times* article of the same time took a similar approach, contrasting the program's "warm, sentimental, humorous" depictions of "the American dream . . . untouched by crime, Cold War or racism" with the harshness of the child actors' real home lives and subsequent challenges as young adults (Margulies 1977). This piece also reveals Chapin's drug addictions in the 1960s, her rehabilitation, and how *Father Knows Best* inspired her to create a loving family with her own two children. It gives voice to Gray's beliefs that "the whole concept of a father knowing best is one that's pretty vulnerable to attack right now" and that the show could have damaged people by giving them false expectations about their lives.

These press pieces not only contrast the 1950s with the 1970s—the latter decade characterized by rising divorce rates, racial discord, generational divides, countercultural ideals, and the women's movement—but their revelations about the child performers' lives at the time of *Father Knows Best* also suggest that the reality of the 1950s was more complicated and seamy than what the series represented. Most of the press accounts and documentaries about the actors or program published or aired between the 1980s and early 2000s are also structured around such contrast and revelations, with the latter impulse given impetus by the 1989 publication of Lauren Chapin's memoir *Father Does Know Best: The Lauren Chapin Story*, which detailed not only the previously revealed narratives about her alcoholic mother and her own drug addiction after the series ended but also her turn to prostitution to support herself, her father's sexual abuse of her, and her eventual religious conversion after achieving sobriety in the 1970s. In the memoir, as well as in all her interviews since the 1970s, Chapin stresses that her "television family"—the *Father Knows Best* cast, especially Robert Young—was more loving and attentive to her than her real family. Although she is active in the group A Minor Consideration, which was founded by former child actor Paul Petersen (who played Jeff on *The Donna Reed Show*) to advocate for the rights of child performers, who are often exploited by both families and the entertainment industry, she also openly expresses her belief that her experience with the cast and crew of *Father Knows Best* was the best of her childhood and that the program's messages about family togetherness were inspirational: "We didn't have that [family love and togetherness] in our real life. . . . I really relied on the Andersons. . . . They taught me that a family should work together to solve problems . . . that to have inner struggles was okay because they could be solved together" ("Daddy's Girls," *Father Knows Best* DVD set).

Like Chapin, actor Billy Gray has articulated an implicit understanding of the role of television, specifically the role of *Father Knows Best*, in educating the public about family and society. However, Gray, who always speaks positively about his fellow cast mates, believes that television, a medium supported by sponsors who "want you to buy what they're selling," has

Lauren Chapin has claimed that working with Young and the rest of
the cast of *Father Knows Best* was the best experience of her childhood.
(Rodney-Young Productions)

negative effects on audiences. He frequently mentions how
some viewers resented his character, Bud, whom they believe
set up real-life parents to have unrealistic expectations for their
sons. Gray is quoted in interviews throughout the 1980s and
1990s as stating that the program "purported to be a reasonable
facsimile of life," but the "dialogue, the situations, the characters
were all totally false. The show did everyone a disservice. . . .
The show contributed to a lot of the problems between men and
women that we see today." He grants that people have received a
"great deal of sustenance from it," but if he could say anything
to make up for the "hoax" of the program, it would be "*you*
know best," a phrase he often uses in autographing photos for
fans (Kisseloff, 344–45; Hall c.1999–2000).

Elinor Donahue, who is the only currently working actor
among the three performers who played the Anderson children,
believes, like Gray, in a positive re-orientation of authority from

the father to the self, but she has had only positive things to say about the program and her role as Betty. She sees the program's representation of gender, as seen through Betty's ambitious character, as not matching the way she thought of herself in the 1950s but as anticipating the social reality of the future, when women would be able to do all the things Betty fought for: "both Betty and Ellie [a working woman character she played on *The Andy Griffith Show* in 1961] were ahead of their time. They certainly tried to get out there and not let gender be an issue. They didn't always succeed, but they made an effort" ("More Liberated Than You Remember" 1993; Rothman 1998). Donahue reads the series of the 1950s through the lens of feminism and sees its idealism as making possible real-life experiences for women in the future.

The actors who played the Anderson children derive their evaluations of the relationship between the program's representations and historical realities from their own experiences as actors and individuals living through the momentous social changes of the last fifty years. Robert Young and Jane Wyatt also addressed the question of the show's "idealism" and "realism" in interviews. By the 1980s–1990s, Young no longer emphasized the program's "realism" as coming from its focus on the small incidents that happen in family life or through its production values. Instead, he offered an implicit understanding of the verisimilitude the program offered viewers; he focused on the tension between the program's "idealistic" representation of the Andersons and the self-recognition that viewers experience from the characters' struggles. In a filmed interview for a special *Father Knows Best* marathon on The Family Channel in 1990, Young said, "We had the audience's understanding and sympathy because they knew what [Jim] was trying to accomplish— the same thing they were trying to accomplish in their lives." To Young, it was the struggles and aspirations of the characters that were recognizable as real, not necessarily the narrative outcomes. In a 1984 *Good Morning, America* cast interview commemorating the thirtieth anniversary of the show's debut, Young was careful to distinguish *real life* from a *sense of reality* that genres can create and confirmed the contract of expectations in which genres and viewers engage. Young recounted how those who derided the show's idealism would recoil when he suggested "next week we're going to do a show in which . . . Kitten is going to develop spinal meningitis. And the following week . . . she is going to die. And they respond, 'oh no!' And I said . . . you wanted reality! . . . This is life, this happens in life." Making no apologies, he explained that the program "was slanted toward humor" and that this "format" meant that only selective aspects of reality were represented.

Jane Wyatt also expressed awareness that the program was following genre and programming conventions that would select and limit what aspects of reality to represent. In reply to a magazine interviewer's comments on the program's "warmth" and "honest sentiment," Wyatt suggested that this was due in part to the happiness that she and Young had experienced in their own families. Yet, "they didn't show all facets of your personality. Margaret really was just in the kitchen all the time, doing things at home, and never seemed to have any outside life. But you can't do very much in a half hour episode." Like Young, she implied that the program created a convincing and still relevant verisimilitude, but in many interviews, she suggested that much of this came from the writing and directing of the characters as distinct individuals, which made them believable. Also, like Young, she suggested there is value in television conventions that present life as "it ought to be." She said, "*We* thought it was real. . . . *We* believed in the family life and we wanted it to be that way" (Amundsen c.1997, 63). Wyatt, recognizing that times have changed since *Father Knows Best*, nevertheless believed that the desire for family life is itself a powerful reality, for "people want to be free, but they still want a nuclear family." Enduring fandom of *Father Knows Best* is a response to that desire (Wyatt, quoted in McLellan, 2006).

Many television programs from the 1950s are subjects of online discussion sites and websites created by fans. "Jeff" of Fatherknowsbest.us, with permission of the Young Family Trust, has crafted a detailed and highly accurate website devoted to the history of *Father Knows Best*, complete with video clips of the openings of the various seasons with original sponsor commercials intact. Many fans and participants in online forums about the series echo the beliefs and attitudes of the actors and journalists. Discussions on one forum, for example, are focused on whether the program is a realistic or idealistic depiction of 1950s' families, whether the program is an appropriate role model for families or television comedies in the present, and whether the program was racist in its exclusion of racial minorities. Some forum participants recount childhoods similar to Chapin's and agree with her assessment that the program offered an inspirationally positive representation of what family love could be like. Other people's remarks are compatible with Gray's opinions about the program's unrealistic expectations for family life, which they believe to be dangerous or delusional. A passionate fan of the program, however, uses his own blog to write an "open letter" to Billy Gray, gently chastising him for his denigration of the program that made him famous and citing his own idyllic experience of childhood and adolescence in the 1950s and 1960s as evidence of Gray's mistake in labeling the program a "hoax."

## Scholarly Critique

Scholarly examinations of *Father Knows Best* often echo aspects of the discursive reconsiderations authored by mainstream journalists and fans—i.e., one of the concerns of media theorists and historians is the relation of the program to "real life." Historians Mary Beth Haralovich and Tasha G. Oren contextualize the program's representations of gender dynamics within the expectations, tensions, and contradictions of 1950s' sociological and media discourses about gender, domestic labor, class, and consumerism. Their stress on "negotiation" as a way to account for the program's process of participating in or reflecting 1950s' social or televisual norms is compatible with my own approach, and they seek to understand *Father Knows Best* and the relevant discourses around it as "documents" of an era rather than evaluating the program as "good" or "bad" for society. In an article repudiating critical approaches to television texts that dismiss mainstream genres, in particular those from the 1950s, as "blissfully ignorant of social conflict," in effect "lulling . . . audience[s] into a dream world where the status quo is the only status," Horace Newcomb and Paul Hirsch use the *Father Knows Best* episode "Betty, Girl Engineer" as an example of how television "does not present firm ideological conclusions—despite its *formal* conclusions—as much as it *comments* on ideological problems" (Newcomb and Hirsch, 565–66). Betty's re-orientation to the domestic sphere at episode's end is not, to these critics, evidence that the arguments she presents for girls in nontraditional roles are to be rejected. In another essay, Newcomb is especially concerned with television accounts that suggest that the dominance of situation comedies, westerns, and detective genres from the mid-1950s to the 1960s represented a "decline" from a "golden age" of early television, when dramatic anthologies provided "serious" treatment of "serious" subject matter. Again, he uses *Father Knows Best* as an example of how genre and programming formulas may have limited how social reality could be represented, but "the brew of social action [of the 1950s] was putting pressure on from the inside" (Newcomb 1997, 119).

While Newcomb, in the latter essay, counterpoises his idea of television as "cultural forum" against only a few key histories of television, his use of *Father Knows Best* to prove the social awareness of 1950s' domestic comedies could function as a rebuttal to a number of scholars who argue that the program portrays America as a "fat, contented place" (MacDonald

99

1985, 109) demonstrates the "ingenuous confidence of a Sunday School film" (Jones 1992, 101) and that it is, in fact, "the sum and substance of . . . benevolent Aryan melodramas" (Marc 1989, 52). Gerard Jones does qualify his smug comparison of the show to a "Sunday School film" by admitting that its representations are "self-contradictory" and representative of a "national confusion" (101). David Marc, however, overreacts in labeling the program "Aryan"—with all its unpleasant political associations—and collapses the series with what is most reactionary and paranoid about 1950s culture, such as the suspicion of "alien cultures" and embrace of consumer capitalism. In his examination of several episodes of the program—against which he elevates the "heroic," critically self-aware comedy of the stand-up comedian—Marc judges *Father Knows Best* to be unfailingly confident, authoritarian, zealous, romantic, static, materialistic, racist, and sexist. While his problem with "Kathy Becomes a Girl," one of the program's most traditional episodes in its enthusiastic rendering of Kathy giving up her "tomboy" identity, seems warranted, Marc describes all episodes centered around dilemmas of the female characters in the same vein—as demonstrations of the program's sexist, authoritarian narrative drive to humiliate women and endorse normative femininity.

The critiques of *Father Knows Best* offered by Nina Liebman, whose *Living Room Lectures* is one of the most developed examination of the 1950s' domestic comedy-melodrama, counter some aspects of Marc's by an attention to how sponsors, the television industry (including self-regulatory standards), and temporal formats limited the kinds of social conflicts that the program could represent. She directly addresses Marc's allegation that the program never depicted vice as she points out how often *Father Knows Best* showed its characters—particularly the children—to be selfish, prideful, and jealous (224). However, she also tends to render all the episodes within a kind of sameness—e.g., according to Liebman, Margaret's "rebellions" are structured to humiliate Margaret and teach her that there will be trouble if she strays outside her role. Although Liebman goes to great lengths to describe the industrial contexts for representational limits, she judges the characters' problems to be "insignificant" in comparison to those of film melodrama characters, with the television laugh track offering viewers a position of superiority that further "trivializes" them (64). She does not consider that the melodramatic structure not only offers viewers "insignificant problems" as stand-ins for larger social ones but also a position that makes visible and touching the disparity between their superior knowledge of the characters' dilemmas and the characters' own limited knowledge, thus enabling viewer empathy rather than scorn.

Jones, Marc, and Liebman grapple with *Father Knows Best*'s powerful evocation of "governance"—its concern with conduct—and suggest that the series either represents the period's imaginative limits about conduct or is itself a tool of the repressive social forces of the era as these have been emphasized in ideological critiques of 1950s' mass media and politics. Anna McCarthy, in her study of corporate-sponsored civic-oriented television programming of the 1950s (ranging from news to arts programming), offers a productive way of thinking about media representations in the postwar period. She argues that the era is characterized by practices that suggest "citizenship . . . is . . . a category of personhood based on some kind of lack, a label describing political subjects who are 'ethically incomplete,' requiring ongoing training and reform if they are truly to live up to the title *citizen*" (McCarthy 2010, 5). The world responded to and made by these citizens is not so much "governed" as characterized by a "will to govern" that emerges out of "contestatory scenes, rife with competing interpretations of human nature and culture" (5–6). These contestatory scenes are evident in both policy decisions and representational practices of specific television programs. If 1950s' America operated under the belief that it was a "consensus society" holding in balance the rights and privileges of interdependent groups, as historian Jennifer Delton argues,

Kathy, a citizen in the making, meets the racial Other in "Family Contest."

its failings are registered in the inability of powerful groups to question the beliefs and justifications that support their privileges (Delton 2013, 6). However, "contestatory scenes" in media representations—or in Attallah's words, disruptions in socially institutionalized discursive hierarchies—negotiate recognition of the rights and interests of others.

From these perspectives, the episode "Family Contest" positions Kathy as a citizen in training. How she acts out her fear that a racially mixed family will get something she wants demonstrates the contradictions produced by television series of the era when they tried to imagine privileged groups struggling to think outside their own interests, which is, in theory, "mandated" by civic participation in the "consensus society." So, while Toby, the Korean orphan, functions as a racial "fetish"— i.e., his "cuteness," evident in his unbridled friendliness and his discursive inadequacies, such as referring to himself in the

third person, functions like a fetish mirroring back to the Andersons their own superiority—the episode also struggles to
encounter his "difference" and re-corporate it into a more plu-
ralistic notion of what constitutes the American family. Kathy's
naturalization of the middle-class, white family as an American
ideal can only be supported and sustained by her "cheating."
When Kathy meets the Other in Toby and recognizes him as a
human invested in his own desire, she repudiates her actions.
The episode demonstrates, perhaps, an overly optimistic and
limited understanding of how white, middle-class privilege can
be shared with others, but its gesture is still significant for a series from this era. The episode, from the program's last first-run
season, ends with the model televisual family of the Andersons
gazing at the photo of an emergent representative American
family that is working class and multi-racial.

1. The term "dramedy" is currently used by many commentators on television to describe programs that combine comedy and drama, but I don't use the term in this study. The term was coined after the period of *Father Knows Best*'s initial run and is used to describe programs as diverse as *Frank's Place* (1987–1988), *The Days and Nights of Molly Dodd* (1987–1991), *Ally McBeal* (1997–2002), and *Enlightened* (2011–2013), as well as others that employ satire, dark comedy, fantasy, and intertextual references, rather than the "heartwarming" humor that *Father Knows Best* combines with drama.

2. See Betty Mills, "Father Knows Best," *TV-Radio Mirror* (February 1956), pp. 56–59, 75–77; Bob Eddy, "Private Life of a Perfect Papa," *Saturday Evening Post* (April 27, 1957), pp. 28–29, 172–73; "Father Still Has His Day . . . because the show wouldn't die," *TV Guide* (June 14–20, 1958), pp. 17–19 for variations on this anecdote.

3. Some historical accounts (Becker 2008, Liebman 1995, Oren 2003, Kassel) discuss the radio version of *Father Knows Best* as if a question mark ended the title; however, the contemporary newspaper and magazine sources on the radio series that I consulted—e.g., profiles of Robert Young, radio schedule listings, program reviews, articles about situation comedies on radio—never list it with the question mark. The misidentification of the title by some scholars may result from an interview with Young reprinted in Kisseloff's *The Box: An Oral History of Television, 1920–1961*. Young states that he and Rodney initially wanted to conclude the title with a question mark, but the sponsor, Kent Cigarettes (Lorillard), refused to support the program if they did. What is confusing in Young's remarks, which are taken out of context from a

longer interview not reprinted by Kisseloff, is whether he is referring to the television or radio version of the program. (Kent only sponsored the television version.) Since it was unlikely that Young and Rodney would have wanted to change the name of the program by adding a question mark when it moved to television, it seems that Young must be referring to the radio version and has misremembered the sponsor. However, whichever media version Young (mis)remembered, primary evidence makes it clear that the program as aired in both media incarnations was never titled *Father Knows Best?*

4. See Christine Becker, *It's the Pictures that Got Small: Hollywood Film Stars on 1950s Television* (Middletown, CT: Wesleyan University Press, 2008) and Mary Desjardins, *Recycled Stars: Female Film Stardom in the Age of Television and Video* (Duke University Press, 2015) for discussions about discourses regarding film stars entering television in the 1940s and 1950s. See Susan Murray, *Hitch Your Antenna to the Stars: Early Television and Broadcast Stardom* (New York: Routledge, 2005) for an examination of what was considered to constitute broadcast stardom during this period.

5. John Caldwell uses *Father Knows Best* as an example of television programming from the 1950s that selectively used cinematic style. He finds it in episodes such as "Hero Father" and "Formula for Happiness," in which Jim's work world is rendered in a visual style reminiscent of film noir but suggests the home setting is portrayed in a style he describes as "zero degree," or "unstylized." However, I would argue that although not every scene in every episode of *Father Knows Best* employs a completely cinematic style—most scenes in each episode, for example, are shot in flat, high-key lighting—almost every episode has one or more scenes in which expressive lighting, deep-focus photography, cinematic actor blocking, etc., are employed. See John Caldwell, *Televisuality: Style, Crisis, and Authority in American Television* (Rutgers University Press, 1995), p. 50.

6. By a popular notion of "classic TV," I am thinking of the campy marketing and programming strategies of cable television's TV Land channel, the nostalgic rerun strategies of cable's The Family Channel or broadcast's MeTV, and the intertextual references of the Hollywood film *Pleasantville* (1999). See Lynn Spigel, *Welcome to the Dreamhouse: Popular Media and Postwar Suburbs* (Durham: Duke University Press, 2001) on how TV Land programming strategies and *Pleasantville* reimagine the role of gender and race in situation comedies of the 1950s.

# BIBLIOGRAPHY

Amundsen, Paul. c.1997. "Mother Knows Best! An interview with Jane Wyatt," *Outré*: 61–66.

Anderson, Christopher. 1994. *Hollywood TV: The Studio System in the Fifties*. Austin: University of Texas Press.

Attallah, Paul. 2003. "The Unworthy Discourse: Situation Comedy in Television," in *Critiquing the Sitcom: A Reader*, ed. Joanne Morreale. Syracuse: Syracuse University Press: 91–115.

Becker, Christine. 2008. *It's the Pictures That Got Small: Hollywood Film Stars on 1950s Television*. Middletown: Wesleyan University Press.

Boddy, William. 1992. *Fifties Television: The Industry and its Critics*. Urbana: University of Illinois Press.

Breines, Wini. 1992. *Young, White and Miserable: Growing Up Female in the Fifties*. Boston: Beacon Press.

Caldwell, John. 1995. *Televisuality: Style, Crisis, and Authority in American Television*. New Brunswick: Rutgers University Press.

Chapin, Lauren, with Collins, Andrew. 1989. *Father Does Know Best: The Lauren Chapin Story*. Nashville: Thomas Nelson Publishers.

Coontz, Stephanie. 2005. *Marriage, a History: How Love Conquered Marriage*. New York: Penguin Books.

———. 1992. *The Way We Never Were: American Families and the Nostalgia Trap*. New York: Basic Books.

"Daddy with a Difference." 1954. *Time*, May 17: 83.

Delton, Jennifer. 2013. *Re-Thinking the 1950s: How Anticommunism and the Cold War Made America Liberal*. New York: Cambridge University Press.

Desjardins, Mary. 2015. *Recycled Stars: Female Film Stardom in the Age of Television and Video*. Durham: Duke University Press.

Eddy, Bob. 1957. "Private Life of a Perfect Papa." *The Saturday Evening Post:* 28–29, 172, 176.

Ehrenreich, Barbara. 1984. *The Hearts of Men: American Dreams and the Flight from Commitment*. New York: Anchor Books.

———, and English, Deirdre. 1978. *For Her Own Good: 150 Years of Experts' Advice to Women*. New York: Doubleday Anchor Books.

Eskenazi, Gerald. 1977. "Keeping Up with 'Father Knows Best.'" *New York Times*, May 15: 93.

Falk, Andrew J. 2010. *Upstaging the Cold War: American Dissent and Cultural Diplomacy, 1940–1960*. Amherst and Boston: University of Massachusetts Press.

"Father Does Know Best: Robert Young Proves a TV Dad Doesn't Have to be Stupid." 1956. *TV Guide*, June 16–22: 8–10.

*Father Knows Best*, Seasons 1–6, DVD. Shout Factory.

"Father Still Has His Day . . . because the show just wouldn't die." 1958. *TV Guide*, June 14–20. Accessed February 24, 2014. fatherknowsbest.us/FKB/Article3.html.

Frazer, June M., and Frazer, Timothy C. 1993. "'Father Knows Best' and 'The Cosby Show': Nostalgia and the Sitcom Tradition." *Journal of Popular Culture* 27:3, 163–73.

Gledhill, Christine. 1987. "The Melodramatic Field: An Investigation," in *Home Is Where the Heart Is: Studies in Melodrama and the Woman's Film*, ed. Christine Gledhill. London: BFI.

Gould, Jack. 1954. "Television in Review: New Comedy." *New York Times*, October 6: 35.

Hall, Ken. c. 1999–2000. "Billy Gray, Bud from *Father Knows Best*, Collects Racing Motorcycles. Accessed August 18, 2014. www.go.star.com/antiquing/billy_gray.htm

Haralovich, Mary Beth. 1992. "Sitcoms and Suburbs: Positioning the 1950s Homemaker," in *Private Screenings: Television and the Female Consumer*, eds. Lynn Spigel and Denise Mann. Minneapolis: University of Minnesota Press.

Hartman, Susan M. 1994. "Women's Employment and the Domestic Ideal in the Early Cold War Years," in *Not June Cleaver: Women and Gender in Post-war America, 1945–60*, ed. Joanne Meyerowitz. Philadelphia: Temple University Press.

"In Review: *Father Knows Best*." 1954. *Broadcasting*, November 8: 14.

Jones, Gerard. 1992. *Honey, I'm Home: Sitcoms: Selling the American Dream*. New York: St. Martin's Press.

Kassell, Michael B. "*Father Knows Best*." *Encyclopedia of Television*. Chicago: Museum of Broadcast Communications. Accessed February 24, 2014. www.musuem.tv/eotv/fatherknows.htm

Kimmel, Michael. 1996. *Manhood in America: A Cultural History*. New York: Free Press.

Kisseloff, Jeff. 1997. *The Box: An Oral History of Television, 1920–61*. New York: Viking.

Kompare, Derek. 2002. "I've Seen This One Before: The Construction of 'Classic TV' on Cable Television" in *Small Screens, Big Ideas: Television in the 1950s*, ed. Janet Thumim. London: I.B. Tauris.

Liebman, Nina. 1995. *Living Room Lectures: The Fifties Family in Film and Television*. Austin: University of Texas Press.

MacDonald, J. Fred. 1985. *Television and the Red Menace: The Video Road to Viet Nam*. New York: Praeger.

Maltin, Leonard. 2008. "Conversations: Robert Young," in *Movie Crazy*. Milwaukie, OR: M Press.

Mannheim, Mannie. 1960. "Is Robert Young Fair to Jane Wyatt?" *Variety*, January 6: 99.

Marc, David. 1989. *Comic Visions: Television Comedy and American Culture*. Malden, MA: Blackwell.

Margulies, Lee. 1977. "17 Years Later . . . Things Father Didn't Know." *Los Angeles Times*, May 13: G1, G16.

McCarthy, Anna. 2010. *The Citizen Machine: Governing by Television in 1950s America*. New York: The New Press.

McLellan, Dennis. 2006. "Jane Wyatt, 96; 'Father Knows Best' Mom," *Los Angeles Times*, October 23: B11.

McLeod, Elizabeth. 2011. Liner notes, *Father Knows Best* CD collection. Little Falls, NJ: Radio Spirits.

Medovoi, Leerom. 2005. *Rebels: Youth Culture and the Cold War Origins of Identity*. Durham: Duke University Press.

Meyerowitz, Joanne. 1994. "Beyond the Feminine Mystique: A Reassessment of Post-war Mass Culture, 1946–58," in *Not June Cleaver: Women and Gender in Post-war America, 1945–60*, ed. Joanne Meyerowitz. Philadelphia: Temple University Press.

Mills, Betty. 1956. "Father Knows Best." *TV-Radio Mirror*. February: 56–59, 75–77.

Monroe, Keith. 1948. "Career Man." *Motion Picture* May: 28–29, 72.

"More Liberated Than You Remember." 1993. *TV Guide*. December 4.

Morreale, Joanne. 2012. *The Donna Reed Show*. Detroit: Wayne State University Press.

Murray, Susan. 2005. *Hitch Your Antenna to the Stars: Early Television and Broadcast Stardom*. New York: Routledge.

Nachman, Gerald. 1998. *Raised on Radio*. Berkeley, CA: University of California Press.

Newcomb, Horace. 1997. "The Opening of America: Meaningful Difference in 1950s America. *The Other Fifties: Interrogating Mid-Century American Icons*, ed. Joel Foreman. Urbana: University of Illinois Press.

———, and Hirsch, Paul. 1987. "Television as a Cultural Forum: Implications for Research," in Television: The Critical View, 4th edition. ed. Horace Newcomb. New York: Oxford University Press.

Oren, Tasha G. 2003. "Domesticated Dads and Double-Shift Moms: Real Life and Ideal Life in 1950s Domestic Comedy." *Cercles* 8: 78–90.

Plant, Rebecca Jo. 2010. *Mom: The Transformation of Motherhood in Modern America*. Chicago: University of Chicago Press.

Remenih, Anton. 1950. "Weekly Radio Drama Praised for its Topics: Father Knows Best How to Tell of Life," *Chicago Daily Tribune*, May 27: C7.

Riesman, David, et al. 1953. *The Lonely Crowd: A Study of the Changing American Character*, abridged edition. New York: Anchor Books.

Rothman, Cliff. 1998. "Sweet Talker." *Los Angeles Times*, December 30: E1, E4.

Shanley, J.P. 1956. "'Father's Start': Robert Young Discusses Origins of His Flourishing Television Program." *New York Times*, August 12: 99.

———. 1955. "TV: Dad is No Dimwit." *New York Times*, March 25: 32.

Shayon, R.L. 1951. "Who Remembers Papa?" *Saturday Review of Literature*, October 13: 43–44.

Sinclair, Charles. 1954. "TV Film Section." *Sponsor*, January 25: 51–59.

Spigel, Lynn. 1992. *Make Room for TV: Television and the Family Ideal in Post-war America*. University of Chicago Press.

———. 2001. *Welcome to the Dreamhouse: Popular Media and Postwar Suburbs*. Durham: Duke University Press.

Taliaferro, Walt. 1949. "Robert Young starts double life with radio family role." *L.A. Daily News*, August 1. Clipping file for Robert Young, Margaret Herrick Library, Academy of Motion Picture Arts and Sciences, Beverly Hills.

Thomas, Deborah. 1988. "Film Noir: How Hollywood Deals with the Deviant Male," *Cinéaction* Summer: 18–28.

Weiss, Jessica. 2000. *To Have and to Hold: Marriage, the Baby Boom, and Social Change.* Chicago: University of Chicago Press.

Whitney, Dwight. 1959. "The Penalty of Being 'Father,'" *TV Guide*, June 20–26: 24–27.

Wolters, Larry. 1954. "Video Flooded with Situation Comedy Series." *Chicago Daily Tribune*, September 19: SW14.

Wyatt, Jane. c.1998–2000. Interview, Archive of American Television. Accessed July 14, 2014. emmytvlegends.org/interviews/shows/father-knows-best